Design for an Empathic World

design
for an
empathic world

Reconnecting People, Nature, and Self

SIM VAN DER RYN

with FRANCINE ALLEN

◑ **ISLAND**PRESS Washington | Covelo | London

Island Press is a trademark of Island Press/The Center for Resource Economics.

Library of Congress Cataloging-in-Publication Data

Van der Ryn, Sim.
  Design for an empathic world : reconnecting people, nature, and self / by Sim Van
der Ryn with Francine Allen.
     pages cm
  Includes bibliographical references and index.
  ISBN-13: 978-1-61091-426-0 (cloth : alk. paper)
  ISBN-10: 1-61091-426-0 (cloth : alk. paper) 1. Human engineering. 2. Architec-
ture--Human factors. 3. City planning--Psychological aspects. I. Title.
  TA166.V35 2013
  720.1'03--dc23
                        2013014321

 Printed on recycled, acid-free paper

Manufactured in the United States of America
10 9 8 7 6 5 4 3 2 1

Keywords: Biological building, biophilia, building metabolism, community-sup-
ported agriculture, ecological design, Farallones Institute, Gaia hypothesis, human-
centered design, indoor air quality, Leadership in Energy and Environmental Design
(LEED), Living Building Challenge, local energy systems, People's Park, Philip Merrill Environmental Center, post-occupancy evaluation, regenerative design, solar
design, University of California Berkeley

*To all of us
who wake up each morning
with gratitude
for the incredible miracle of life
and the happiness it brings to us
and everyone we touch.*

Vineyards—Sonoma

Contents

Crestone—Colorado

Preface

A Journey to Connect with the Natural World

BEFORE MY FIFTH BIRTHDAY, my parents, my brother and sister and I left our comfortable home in the Netherlands and sailed first to London and then to New York. We left shortly before the Nazi invasion of our country. My parents left large families behind and it would be five years before they learned that few friends or family had survived the Holocaust. I was too young to understand the grief and pain they could not share with us.

I often felt uncomfortable in our fourth-floor apartment in New York and would spend every spare moment after school and on weekends in the ragged bits of nature in our neighborhood: patches of sumac and marshes, and the rough ground along the railroad, where I visited a Shinnecock Indian–African American who lived in a piano crate near the tracks.

The cultivation and collection of living things, the wonder of and being in nature grounded my inner self. In the bedroom I shared with my scientist brother, I raised hamsters and tropical fish, and collected snakes and aquatic insects I caught in a local marsh. One day while my mother was scrubbing the floors, a snake slithered onto her leg. That was the end of my bedroom zoo.

During high school summer breaks, I worked on New England farms, where I had my first building experiences that led me into architecture. During summer break in my college years in Ann Arbor, I would drive to the Rockies and the desert. When my new bride and I moved to California in 1958, we would explore the wild coast and the Sierra foothills on weekends. A few years later when I started teaching at Berkeley, I'd spend weeks each summer hiking alone in the Sierra.

Berkeley in the sixties was an exciting and stimulating place to live and work. In 1961, I joined the architecture faculty at the University of California. My major interest was in research on how people respond to the designed environments they live and work in, and how this information could inform the design process.

The sixties were also very traumatic times, both on the campus and throughout the nation. President John F. Kennedy, his brother Robert, and Martin Luther King Jr. were assassinated. A robust student and faculty movement grew out of the UC Berkeley administration's refusal to allow free speech on campus to groups recruiting students to participate in civil rights work in the South. Hundreds were arrested. In the spring of 1969, Governor Reagan invaded the campus and the city with National Guard soldiers and helicopters to take back a vacant piece of university land that the community had turned into a park (see chapter 4).

The trauma of an armed invasion of the nation's leading public university, the daily news of the violent deaths of innocent Vietnamese by our troops, the dashed hopes of JFK's New Frontier, and my personal memories of our flight from Europe thirty years earlier converged in my inner being, telling me, "It's time to leave this place." We left our home in Berkeley in 1969 and moved into a small cabin I'd built a few years earlier in a wooded ridge on the Point Reyes peninsula, surrounded by Point Reyes National Seashore. The national seashore, established in 1962, is over 71,000 acres of forest and grassland cattle ranches, beautiful isolated pristine beaches on the ocean and the bay, abutting a ranching town on the mainland, and a quaint village of summer homes nearby. I received a Guggenheim grant in 1971 to write a book about the work we had been doing in Berkeley elementary schools to incorporate design and building into the classroom environment in 1968–1970, so I took a leave from teaching. During the year in Point Reyes, my kids and I, with help from a few former Berkeley students, started patching together the book on the floor of the cabin.

Life on this remote ridge was very different from our life in Berkeley. Clock time seemed to stand still as days rolled by. Slowly we got to meet other people who'd escaped to this place. The urban and national chaos of those times created a large "back-to-the-land movement" and many experiments in new forms of community, which I was studying and documenting through a grant from the National Institute of Mental Health. I visited communes in the Southwest and California where the use of psychedelic drugs was common, and often led to the collapse of these experiments.

LSD had been brought to North America by Dr. Humphrey Osmond, a British psychiatrist who tested it as a cure for schizophrenia in Canadian hospitals and also in a Veterans Administration hospital in Palo Alto, California, the inspiration for Ken Kesey's novel *One Flew Over the Cuckoo's Nest* and many other adventures in those wild days. The English author Aldous Huxley wrote about his experiences with the drug in *The Doors of Perception.*

Back at our secluded refuge, I took my first and only LSD trip alone in the remote forests and beaches, in an altered state of consciousness that lasted for hours. My thinking mind stopped working. My eyes, breath, and heartbeat absorbed all the details in the life around me as my skin and body seemed to melt and merge with the birds, bugs, grass, trees, leaves, sun, wind, water, and sound. It was a profound, deep experience that I did not need to repeat.

Years later, as I sat with Gregory Bateson (author of *Mind and Nature* and *Steps to an Ecology of Mind*)[1] during the last days of his life, he recited this verse to me:

> *Men are alive. Plato is a man. Plato is alive.*
> *Men are alive. Grass is alive. Men are grass.*

I nodded and smiled. He told the ultimate truth. The logic of nature is that all life is part of a single cooperating whole, a truth that the modern world needs to wake up to soon, if our species is to continue living on Earth. Prevalent ideologies continue to insist that humankind is above and separate from nature. Neither science nor reason will persuade those who cannot feel the truth in their hearts to discover their hidden center and inner selves.

I'm grateful to my parents for having had the strength and foresight to leave behind family and friends, to sacrifice a comfortable life, homeland, income, and position, to leave Europe after the Nazi invasion of Poland and come to a strange new country and make new lives. I'm grateful for the kind and gentle teachers, mentors, and employers who patiently guided the boy and young man who peppered them with difficult questions, challenging the existing rules. They encouraged me to follow my own path. I am grateful to my first wife, who always supported me in my idiosyncratic journey and was always a patient and loving mother to our three children. I'm grateful to our children, who endured the difficult times and have all gone on to happiness and success in their lives. I'm grateful to friends and colleagues who worked with me over the years for their loyalty and great work. I'm grateful for the wonderful clients with whom I was able to share similar values and visions to achieve their dreams and my own. I'm grateful to live in a place of great natural peace and beauty, a community with so many remarkable folk. I'm grateful to the higher powers that have sustained me even when I could not recognize them, and I'm grateful that they brought my precious beloved and me together. I'm grateful for the miracle of life and all it brings to us.

I want to thank the Rockefeller Foundation for providing support to write this book and for honoring me with a second Bellagio Residency in 2013. Dusan Mills, an old client and friend, generously spent days photographing hundreds of my watercolors, some of which appear in this book. Aran Baker, an artist, designer, and planner with chemical sensitivities, researched and conducted interviews with experts on healthy building that are incorporated into chapter 2. Josiah Cain, an inspired landscape architect and ecological designer, provided notes on bringing nature into cities that are included in chapter 3. Every day at Yoga Toes Studio, my teacher, Amanda Giacomini, grounded my body and soul through the months it took to write this book. The book wouldn't be here without Francine, my partner in life, who encouraged me to write it, providing the emotional and intellectual support at every step with her own years of experience as a teacher, writer, and editor. Heather Boyer, to whom I had sent an earlier book proposal composed of a collection of my essays, which was not of interest to Island Press, then encouraged me to develop a new book proposal. Through a series of long e-mail exchanges, Heather and I were partners in shaping the form and content of *Design for an Empathic World*. I am grateful for her trust and expertise.

Foreword

A Sustained Awakening of the Human Heart

What is essential is invisible to the eye.

—*Antoine de Saint-Exupéry*

FEW PEOPLE IN THE SUSTAINABLE DESIGN FIELD have had as significant and enduring impact as Sim Van der Ryn. For several decades now Sim has been leading the green-building movement, writing, speaking, and building examples of a better, more regenerative future. He is one of our sages—providing counsel on the possibilities and ramifications of our design decisions, telling us inspiring stories for change, and building the models that prove what is possible. His books are essential reading to anyone interested in understanding a truly sustainable future.

For me personally, Sim has been an essential guidepost. My work with the Living Building Challenge, the world's most progressive and stringent green-building program (www.living-future.org) would not be what it is without some early inspiration gleaned from *The Integral Urban House* and *The Toilet Papers*, both of which were hugely important in shaping my views toward integration and ecology. *Ecological Design*, published in the early nineties, is still one of the publications I recommend most to individuals starting their career in this important field.

I remember early in my own career, thumbing through an old, moldy copy of *The Integral Urban House* and thinking that within these pages were solutions to many of the problems our society was currently facing. At that point the book was out of print, but regardless had found its way to me at the right place and the right time. Things seem to happen for a reason sometimes.

Over the years I have had the opportunity to get to know Sim and to hear his wisdom and teachings firsthand. He taught me to rethink the very concept of waste and to always think in terms of healthy, diverse, and interconnected systems. Perhaps my obsession with the composting toilet is owed to him as well. I have become enriched by his ideas and by his friendship.

And now with this book, Sim focuses on the most important understanding of all, that *the only thing that can truly save us is a sustained awakening of the human heart.*

Over the last few years I have watched the green-building movement explode with interest and move from a fringe idea to one discussed as part of nearly every commercial project. Too often I have witnessed buildings built that use slightly less energy and resources than their conventional counterparts, lavishly adorned with green bling and gold plaques, yet failing to inspire or to engender any systemic change. I have seen sustainability branded as a marketing term or as justification for mostly questionable thinking. It is tough when beautiful words like ecological and green get co-opted and co-joined with the same lack of spirit that has been diminishing the planet for so many years.

And yet I have also seen firsthand the real difference that exists when there is a deep understanding and empathy for life and community, when some mystery ingredient has been added that elevates the project and all those involved. More important than any green technology or certification system is the sensitivity and caring evident by those designing—empathy!

As Sim discusses in this book, when there is a love of place, indeed, a love of life manifest in our actions and armored by our passionate intent, we have the capacity to be a powerful healing species and not merely the destructive species of the last couple centuries. We can create places worthy of their resources that can endure and create more opportunities for biodiversity and life while serving as our habitat. The keyword being *our*—part of a larger intergenerational and interspecies sharing of resources instead of co-opted and selfish resource use.

This message is the thing that this delightful book focuses on—the idea that outward regeneration requires an inner regenerative spirit as precondition and the sobering reality that the environmental crisis is but an outer manifestation of our own personal and societal inner crisis. This crisis has at its root an extreme disconnect with the systems and elements that sustain us—a disconnect with life, our own life and the lives of everything else around us. It is a sad and lonely realization. As such it is only through empathy that we can reconnect and see our rightful place as part of life, not separate, superior, or so very alone.

This realization can lead us to build habitat for our species that can serve as an ecotone for other species, like reefs in the ocean, harboring greater productivity and abundance, color, beauty, life.

Empathic design as practice is a critical resource offered by our wise sage of the green-building movement at the right time, when so much interest in the topic is finally here. For new students of architecture, planning, and engineering, it is essential that they learn *what is essential* and be exposed to and encouraged to get in touch with the profound beauty that is life. For longer practitioners, this book serves as a powerful reawakening.

While this is not a big book, it is large beyond its size. It reminds us of what is essential, it tells us a story of where key ideas to the green-building movement came from, and teaches us about the key principles that need to guide and shape architecture and the built environment into the future. I am honored and humbled to have the opportunity to invite you to delve inside.

—*Jason F. McLennan*

CEO, International Living Future Institute, and
Winner of the Buckminster Fuller Prize

North of Taos

Desertscape—New Mexico

Watercolors

THE ART IN THIS BOOK CONSISTS OF WATERCOLORS I PAINTED AS PART OF MY DISCOVERY of self—part of the process of reconnecting to others and to nature. For me, painting is a meditation on nature, recording what I see, and using this fluid technique to quickly capture my impressions of the essence of nature wherever I am. An early lesson I learned was not to paint "objects" but to focus on overall form, on where one edge meets another. The half hour to an hour of sitting in stillness while painting in place is a form of meditation, connecting to the inner self and a natural setting focused only on the present.

In the late 1980s, the chairman of UC Berkeley's architecture department invited me to teach a watercolor painting course and I gratefully accepted. The all-day class, Watercolor Sketching Outdoors, was held off campus on Fridays. I chose favorite places in the Bay Area: waterfront, quiet cemeteries, Napa Valley, out-of-the-way older neighborhoods. Many students seldom got away from the campus. I saw this class as an opportunity for them to slow down and relax their minds. I emphasized to them that seeing is different from looking. Looking is the activity of an outsider peering in, while seeing comes from inside, from absorbing the place and the present moment. I had a firm rule that there would be no talking during class. In this class, I gave no instructions. Sometimes I did a brief demonstration before we all began to paint, but I did not critique their work. I still hear from students whose lives and careers were changed by that learning experience, which allowed them to see as well as nurture the inner self. By learning to paint outside of ego and the judgments of others, which constrict and short-circuit the experience of a larger inner self, they found their own truth and sense of peace.

Phelps Barn – St Helena

Phelps Winery—St. Helena, California

Sierras—California

1 | Introduction

> *The salvation of the human world lies nowhere*
> *else than in the human heart, in the human power*
> *to reflect, in human modesty, and in human re-*
> *sponsibility.*
>
> *—Václav Havel*

IN THE FALL OF 2008 after the beginnings of the financial meltdown on Wall Street, I started getting frantic calls and e-mails from both young and seasoned architects who'd been laid off and also a smaller number of communications from people who worked on Wall Street—mostly young but also some more senior people. I'm not sure why they contacted me—the architects might have known about me or read my books—certainly not the Wall Streeters, whom I did ask, "Why are you calling me?" Their answer was that they were referred to me by mutual friends.

My response took me back to backpacking experiences. Occasionally, when I was backpacking alone in western wilderness mountain areas, I would get lost. I had maps but GPS was yet to be invented. My first response was panic. Then I would sit down quietly and breathe slowly into my core, a place I now call "the inner self"—a sanctuary to go into when one is in difficult times. I would breathe, shut down my frantic mind, and follow the wordless intuition, which emerged from deep within my core.

My reply to those who contacted me was, "When you feel lost, throw away your mental maps and find a safe place, a sanctuary within yourself where your deepest self and inner truth lives." Some of my correspondents would stutter and end the conversation right there. Others would ask if they could visit me at my home on the rural coast of Northern California, and I met with quite a few.

I suddenly found myself acting as a life guide. Why was I willing to do this? I'm a member of the "Lucky Generation" born during the Great Depression of the 1930s who came into the workforce in the 1950s as America began a period of tremendous expansion and growth following World War II. When I graduated with a bachelor's degree in architecture from the University of Michigan in 1958, I had lots of job offers, and not because I had been an exceptional student. Gordon Bunshaft, chief of design at Skidmore Owings and Merrill, then the top corporate firm in the country, offered me a job in New York. Touring the drafting room, I was dazed by the sight of more than a hundred men in white shirts and ties hunched over their drafting boards.

This was not for me. I flew to San Francisco and found many smaller offices that were hiring. After a few years completing my internship, I started teaching in the architecture program at the University of California, Berkeley, and also started an office with a high school friend from New York, Sanford Hirshen. In my academic career, I was mentored in my work by department chairs and deans who were very supportive of my interests, even though they didn't fit into the mainstream architectural program at the

Fireboat—San Francisco

time. Our young firm did significant work in low-cost and innovative housing and we had great clients.

When the calls came in from desperate young architects in 2008, I knew it was time to do what I could for other designers who did not live in a time as generous, optimistic, and supportive of innovation as my contemporaries and I had.

I feel gratitude toward an empathic older generation that nurtured and guided me as a young architect and teacher. My generation and the post–World War II baby boomers that followed have the opportunity to enable today's younger generation in their lives, which are more difficult than ours were. That is a task we should be grateful to accept as our legacy to a younger generation. As we get older, we hopefully feel ourselves more deeply living the truth of our inner selves; and sharing that with a new generation is something we can give to those who will follow us.

In this book, I share my thoughts and experience about the design of our world today. I focus on both the strengths and the weaknesses in our approach to the design of our communities, regions, and buildings with a critical eye and suggest how we can help create a better world for others and ourselves. Mine has been a long journey. As Steve Jobs said, "You can only connect [the dots] looking backwards."[1] The biggest lessons I've learned relate to caring for others and being true to myself. Carlos Casteneda once said, "Look at every path closely and deliberately, then ask ourselves this crucial question: Does this path have a heart? If it does, then the path is good. If it doesn't then it is of no use to us."[2]

My lifetime focus has been shifting the paradigm in architecture and design. We now think of design primarily in relation to the infrastructure we live in and with: buildings, transportation, automobiles and highways, trains and buses, airplanes and airports, oil and natural gas lines, electricity, water and sewer systems, phones, computers, TV and radios. There is little focus on the people who use and are affected by this infrastructure. There is still little thought given within design professions to how someone will use a space or a building. The design brief or program is generally prepared by the client and defined mostly in terms of square foot requirements for different uses. Basically, design leaves out any real understanding of human ecology or end-user preferences. How many office workers would voluntarily choose to spend their working lives in windowless cubicles? Although it seems like common sense, the field of post-occupancy evaluation that I helped to found in the 1970s is still not broadly accepted. Post-occupancy evaluation uses observation and interviews as tools to uncover how occupants actually use and respond to the designed environments they live and work in.

This disconnect from end use allows designers to design without empathy for humans, to separate the work from themselves, and still too often, to design without empathy for the natural environment. It is not just one of these connections, but all three—to self, to others, and to nature—that are necessary to design for a future that is more humane, equitable, and resilient.

At a time when the gap between the wealthy and the poor is expanding, we're faced with the possibility of peak oil, increasing incidents of human-induced as well as natural disasters (many as a result of or exacerbated by climate change), and challenges to strong in-person community networks brought about by more time in cyberspace than public space. We need to takes steps to reconnect design to the human and natural elements that are being lost at great expense. Design is much more than ratios, regulations, and beautiful 3D models. The way we approach design has implications for human and natural networks and the future of our planet.

Integrating the design of human systems and natural systems for the benefit of humans and the living world is ecological design, an important addition to our design toolbox. (This is the topic of one of my earlier books, *Ecological Design*, with Stuart Cowan.[3]) But including the very important integration of connection to humans (self and others) is what I am calling empathic design. Empathy is learned and practiced through direct experience and awareness that there is life beyond the physical, material world.

A silent player in design is the structure of the human brain, which has not changed since humans joined the earth. Our brains are wired so we can instantly respond to immediate short-term threats, but not to long-term threats that we cannot experience directly. Empathic design implies thinking ahead, integrating probable future risks such as oceans rising, temperatures rising, soils declining in fertility, chemical pollution of water. Empathic design should consider both the precautionary principle as well as the law of unintended consequences.

Many people are not aware they have an inner self that shelters their deepest truths. We live in a fast-moving information-overload culture where people are encouraged to project their image of themselves, their persona—in the workplace and through social media.

MIT technology scientist Sherry Turkle's book *Alone Together: Why We Expect More from Technology and Less from Each Other* takes a hard look at how new technologies designed to bring us closer together are driving us further from each other and from ourselves.[4] We don't find our deeper inner selves on our smart phones, texting, social networks, or in Internet conferences.

I'm not suggesting that we return to the Stone Age, but that we understand the implications of technology on design and community. New technology has provided enormous benefits to design and facilitated the creation of communities online as well as in person. But online communities and our thirst for a constant stream of information on a device should not replace human interaction. It was the mechanization of the world that separated design from its human and natural roots, and part of the reason design is now faced with a pressing need to become more humane—to become empathic.

Spring—Bellagio, Italy

When did design enter the human story? Early humans made simple tools of stone and wood to pound plants and seeds to eat, kill game for food, skin animal hides for clothing, make fire, and paint themselves and their caves with pictures of animals. Agriculture is the mother of architecture. Agriculture created hierarchical systems of power and control that served wealth and power, and five thousand years later, that is still architecture's major purpose and client base.

Sigfried Giedion's monumental work *Mechanization Takes Command* meticulously examines the history of mechanization and its effects.[5] He begins with designs to eliminate handcraft in building, agriculture, and homemaking. He recounts the development of the mass assembly line, created first to disassemble pigs and cattle, and later to assemble automobiles. The book was published in 1948, before today's totally computerized robotic assembly lines. The larger picture we are left with is that the design of the nineteenth- and twentieth-century Industrial Revolution resulted in the disassembly of the living organic world and the assembly of a mechanical world.

How do we reassemble or reconnect the built world to the human and natural worlds? Change in our design professions and practice, and in all of our institutions will come when enough people have empathy for other people and all forms of life. In Carlos Castaneda's *The Teachings of Don Juan,* Don Juan instructs his students to walk as long as it takes in the desert until they find their spot, the place where they feel truly at home. I used this same approach in community design projects located in natural landscapes, instructing participants to walk in silence until they found the place that felt best to them. Usually, after some hours, we'd find people clustered in the same place—an example of discovering an empathic relation between self and place in nature.

In this book I do not address specific solutions for reforming society's institutions. My hope is that my journey and experience can provide inspiration and a path for moving toward more empathic design.

I follow this chapter with a focus on the practice of human-centered design, which was very much in focus during the social revolution of the 1960s and since then largely neglected. Following that, I explore design education, its strengths and weaknesses, and call for integrating hands-on design experiences early into a child's education. Next, I discuss nature-centered design, which is finally being welcomed as vital to responsible design today. That leads to a discussion of the possible opportunities for moving toward more empathic design. I close with a view of the journey toward one's inner self, where we each find our deepest truth and fullest heart.

I hope that this book will inspire collaboration within and across disciplines—that it will help to foster the collaboration and thoughtfulness necessary to achieve a more empathic future.

Ernest Callenbach, the author of *Ecotopia*, who died in the spring of 2012, left a wise and beautiful epistle on his computer shortly before his death. These excerpts capture the challenges and the hope for our future. "We are facing a century or more of exceedingly difficult times. . . . We live in a dark time here on our tiny precious planet. Ecological devastation, political and economic collapse, irreconcilable ideological and religious conflict, poverty, famine: the end of the overshoot of cheap oil based consumer capitalist expansionism. . . . How will those who survive manage it? What can we teach our friends, our children, our communities? Although we may not be capable of chang-ing history, how can we equip ourselves to survive it? Hope.

Children exude hope, even under the most terrible conditions, and that must inspire us as our conditions get worse. . . . Mutual support. The people who do best at basic survival skills are co-operative, good at teamwork, altruistic, mindful of the common good. . . . Thinking together is enormously creative; it has huge survival value."[6]

Generator and boat hauling winch—Sausalito Waterfront

2 | Human-Centered Design

The fight is never about grapes or lettuce. It is always about people.

—*Cesar Chavez*

IN 1964, PRESIDENT JOHNSON PUSHED THROUGH the Economic Opportunity Act, the centerpiece of the War on Poverty. Governor Pat Brown appointed Dr. Paul O'Rourke, a longtime advocate for improving farmworker living conditions, as director of the new agency, California Office of Economic Opportunity. O'Rourke chose as its highest priority improving housing, health care, and child care for migrant farm labor families in California's Central Valley, where most of the US vegetable crops are grown. He retained my partner Sanford Hirshen and me to plan, design, and build facilities for migrant farmworker housing, health and child care in twenty-two rural counties. There were no building codes for farmworker housing. How could you write a code for families camping out under a bridge, sleeping in their cars, or living in an abandoned shack where a labor contractor stuffed as many workers as possible? Our assignment was not only to design and build the facilities, but also to find and secure the sites, which neither the counties nor the farmers were eager to provide. The industry needed tens of thousands of workers during the growing season and harvest times, but they didn't want them living in their backyards.

We searched for suitable building systems for both housing and separate health care and child care facilities. We also had to design infrastructure for each 100-home camp, including electricity, water, and sewer lines. We came up with a simple, straightforward system for the homes. We took two sheets of plywood, bonded them to a two-inch slab of Styrofoam, placed a two-by-four at either end, and we had a simple sturdy system for walls and roof. We didn't know it at the time, but we had invented the first version of what are now known as SIP, or structurally integrated panels, and widely used in high-performance building projects. We provided each family with living and sleeping space, bath, and kitchen at a cost of less than $5 per square foot.

Between 1964 and 1974, we designed and built thirty-three camps to shelter migrant farmworkers and their families in California. Sargent Shriver, President Kennedy's brother-in-law and director of the nationwide OEO program, and Robert Kennedy both visited the camps with great interest. Farmworker leader Cesar Chavez was in favor of farmworkers developing their own communities, and we supported that effort. Yet, forty years later, in spite of these efforts and interest from high-profile political figures, the lack of suitable housing, health care, and child care for service workers remains a largely unresolved problem across the country. While advances have been made in some aspects of human-centered design, more significant changes in the field of architecture may be necessary to become truly empathic.

Richard Farson, a psychologist, founder of the California Institute of the Arts and former board member of the American Institute of Architects, forthrightly addresses the issue of architects' seeming unwillingness to become advocates for users of their products. In his 2008 book *The Power of Design*, which was praised by many leaders in the design fields, Farson asks, "Is design a profession or a business? I think most designers would answer 'both' because they are not aware of the differences, let alone any ethical incompatibility between the two. Because in recent years architecture and design have become far more business than profession and because designers believe the corporate world is where their financial futures lie, they have come to share the values of that world. No longer do they expect to fulfill the social responsibilities they may once have cared about most. The results of our designs almost always affect the public, and so the consequences of any such compromise are actually borne by the public. As currently practiced, architecture and design are not essential because they are more business than profession."[1]

His is a powerful indictment from a leading psychologist who has partnered with the architecture profession to help it reach its full potential. Correcting the failed structure of the design process so that users are valued participants from the start, having clearly stated design strategies on how users will be served, and then objectively and systematically evaluating the project when it is occupied to see what worked and what didn't, is the only way design will get smarter, more effective, and empathic. Almost fifty years after the field of post-occupancy evaluation was created, with positive results for users, it remains a powerful, unused strategy to improve the human environment.

I began my post-occupancy evaluation studies by developing a series of methods to study user behavior in designed spaces through observation, interviews, questionnaires, and activity logs kept by users. In the late 1960s, students in my graduate seminar and I had undertaken an environmental analysis of a pinwheel of four high-rise dormitories a block from the campus. Our focus was on the actual behaviors and preferences of the silent partner in any design process—the user who has to live with untested design assumptions.

We were concerned with developing an approach to architectural programming that went beyond a specification of square footage requirements for various building types. What we documented through deep participatory observation and interviews with dorm residents was that the long-held assumptions of administrators and architects were inconsistent with the actual preferences and activities of student dorm living.

As I wrote in a 1967 article in *Architectural Forum*, "Administrators have been so preoccupied with problems of growth, cost, and budgets that basic assumptions of student housing design have seldom been questioned. There is no feedback: existing facilities have not been systematically evaluated as to whether they are effectively providing the kind of environment students want and need. The emphasis of our study was on evaluating qualitative aspects of student housing. We tried to go beyond quantitative measures of building performance such as temperature, lighting levels, and noise control, to develop an approach to architectural programming that went beyond a catalog of square footage. . . . Our focus was on the silent partner in the design process—the user affected by design decisions."[2]

The dorm project received acclaim from architectural critics and awards from the American Institute of Architects. Out of the monograph resulting from our work, "Dorms at Berkeley: An Environmental Analysis," the new field of post-occupancy evaluation developed, and also a new professional organization that is still active, the Environmental Design Research Association (EDRA), which includes both designers and social scientists.[3]

These early studies did result in significant changes in student housing design. As a result of our interviews with dorm students, and on-site observation, we proposed a new student housing model to replace the high-rise hotel: a cluster of four to six single-occupancy rooms with a shared common room, kitchen, and bath—a flexible shared apartment. Two- and three-storied student apartment clusters proved far less expensive to build and at the same or higher density than the high-rises. They became a preferred student housing choice on many campuses, while vacancy rates in the high-rise-hotel model rose significantly.

An ally and mentor in this work was Martin Trow, a social scientist at Berkeley who spent his long career studying all aspects of higher education, including how buildings on campuses were actually used, what worked and what didn't. He suggested in an essay on architecture and education, "Perhaps the most fruitful form of investigation could be simply looking at how people use space, successfully or unsuccessfully, through a kind of participant observation. This is very rare, in part because it does not look like work or science."[4]

Trow touches on what he calls "the pathologies of institutional planning" and cites a host of familiar issues. "In most institutions, there is a considerable division of labor in the organization of physical planning, a remoteness in the decision making process that goes on very far away from the body of potential users." He writes, "The process is enveloped in unbelievable clouds of obscurity . . . . there's a vague 'offstage' that establishes certain conditions, understandings and assumptions . . . . the consequence is that the planning of space and use of space are separated geographically and socially by quite a lot of distance."[5]

Following the dorm project, I went on to conduct studies of courtrooms and correctional facilities. In 1975, Governor Jerry Brown appointed me California State Architect responsible for managing the state's design and construction program, with a staff of hundreds and an annual budget in the hundreds of millions of dollars. Jerry Brown's great gift to government was to appoint outsiders rather than the usual insiders to run every state agency. I reserved 1 percent of the budget of each project for a post-occupancy evaluation (POE) of that project after a year of occupancy. It was not to be. My client agencies—the prison system, parks, general services, motor vehicle department, and others—would not agree to POE. They were afraid that if we found that facilities didn't work as they had expected, it would reflect negatively on their bureaucracy. At the same time, important POE studies of public housing by Clare Cooper Marcus at Berkeley (*Easter Hill Village: Some Social Implications of Design*, 1975),[6] Oscar Newman (*Defensible Space: Crime Prevention Through Urban Design*, 1973),[7] and Jane Jacobs (*The Death and Life of Great American Cities*, 1961)[8] produced major shifts in the design of everything from communities to federal public housing, leading to the dramatic dynamiting of the large Pruitt-Igoe project in Saint Louis and others in major urban areas. These efforts at destroying high-rise housing for poor people were a disaster because the displaced families were then forced into older rundown slum housing. Although a whole new field of study, crime prevention through environmental design (CPTED), became an established field of research in the 1970s, it didn't address the fundamental issue of designing appropriate housing for the disenfranchised.

Today there is great opportunity to integrate the ideas of post-occupancy evaluation into the very successful rating systems for green buildings and neighborhoods. The LEED (Leadership in Environmental and Energy-efficient Design) rating system created by the US Green Building Council (USGBC) is one of the ways in which "green" "healthy" design has been advanced most effectively in the United States. USGBC is always expanding and improving the rating system, and one area of improvement under consideration is building performance over time. I have for many years suggested that USGBC certification should be based on a building's actual performance rather than on design assumptions.

In 2006, the Cascadia Green Building Council conducted a detailed analysis of ten buildings built to LEED standards in the Portland, Oregon, area. Its summary analysis reports, "This study's limited sample suggests that design modeling rarely comes within 10% of actual energy utilization levels. . . . User surveys show a higher percentage of occupants were dissatisfied with light levels and sound privacy in green buildings than in baseline buildings. Our results suggest a need for improvements in controllability of lighting, and innovative strategies to accommodate sound privacy needs in open plan or cubicle office layouts in both comparison groups."[9] Regarding actual energy use, the study showed that three of the buildings performed close to design assumptions, four used less energy than design assumptions, and three used more energy—in the worst case, three times the projected energy use.

USGBC is in the early stages of instituting a recertification program for the 35,000 to 45,000 LEED-certified buildings around the world that they say will include an assessment of "human experience," including factors such as thermal comfort, acoustics and air quality, lighting, office layout and furnishings. This information will likely be collected in the same way as our UC Berkeley study (described below), which used e-mail questionnaires of building users.

The Center for the Built Environment (CBE) at UC Berkeley did a pioneering post-occupancy evaluation of a LEED Platinum building in Annapolis, Maryland, during four months of 2004. The Philip Merrill Environmental Center, which serves as the headquarters for the Chesapeake Bay Foundation, opened in 2001, so the study reflects four years of use. According to the Chesapeake Bay Foundation, "the center and its sophisticated systems have won international acclaim as a model for energy efficiency, high performance, and water conservation."[10]

In the executive summary of the report, UC Berkeley researchers say: "It is widely believed that sustainable building design strategies create improved indoor environmental quality and should, thus, be associated with improved occupant comfort, satisfaction, health, and work performance relative to buildings designed around standard practices. Yet, this belief remains a hypothesis with little empirical support. The study described in this report represents a beginning step in understanding the human factors impacts of sustainable design practices."[11]

The specific findings in the Merrill Center study, both positive and negative, can help to inform future green-building projects that will have greater benefit to the end user. The most frequently cited concerns were temperature conditions, noise distractions, insufficient meeting rooms, and glare from windows. The most frequently cited positive factors were the connection to nature and the bay, the access to daylight and views, the openness of the space, the lunchroom, and the overall aesthetics of the building. The findings from the Occupant Indoor Environmental Quality survey, interviews, and discussion groups showed that 74 percent of the comments were of a positive nature, and 27 percent were about concerns or problems.

Specific findings include the following:

- Occupants were highly satisfied with the Merrill Center building as a whole. In fact, the score for overall building satisfaction was the second highest in the entire CBE survey database.

- Satisfaction with air quality was very positive and represents the highest level of air quality satisfaction in the CBE database.

- Close to 90 percent of the occupants were satisfied with daylighting, the overall amount of light, and access to views.

- Ratings for the psychosocial outcomes were positive, with about 80 percent of the occupants experiencing high levels of morale, well-being, and sense of belonging at work.

- Occupants have a strong sense of pride in the building, as indicated by the fact that 97 percent of survey respondents said they were proud to show the office to visitors.

- Acoustical conditions were the most negatively rated, primarily due to distractions from people talking and loss of speech privacy associated with the highly open environment. Even so, the acoustics score was well above average in comparison with the CBE database.

Findings from the interviews and focus groups also provide insights about the psychosocial benefits of the building. Psychological benefits included sense of pride in the values conveyed by the building, a more positive overall workplace experience, and a strong connection to the natural environment. Social benefits included improved communication and sense of belonging as well

Big Sur Coast

as feelings of being treated in an egalitarian manner, especially regarding access to benefits of daylight and views. Participants in the interviews and focus groups also felt that the building very strongly conveyed the mission and values of the Chesapeake Bay Foundation. As one senior executive pointed out, the building's location on the edge of the bay allows everyone to "see what we are working on and what we are working for."[12]

At UC Berkeley's College of Environmental Design in the 1960s, there was a small group of faculty whose concern was human-centered design. We began systemic studies of built environments to uncover how they functioned in terms of human ecology—the interaction of a building's users with the designed environment they lived or worked in. Roslyn Lindheim studied hospital environments, Clare Cooper Marcus studied public housing, Henry Sanoff studied low-cost housing in equatorial climates, Christopher Alexander and his students were developing a "pattern language" of design features at various scales and how they connected to people's needs and wants. Psychologist Robert Sommer at UC Davis studied institutional environments. Richard Farson tells the story of Robert Sommer's work in *The Power of Design*. "More than four decades ago, the young social psychologist Robert Sommer noted that patients of a psychiatric hospital in which he worked sat silently on benches facing each other across a wide hallway. He decided to redesign the area into what looked more like a sidewalk cafe, with small tables and chairs so that the patients sat at right angles to each other, a more conversational arrangement. The behavior change was dramatic. His now classic studies showed the increased interaction proved highly beneficial."[13]

Clare Cooper Marcus in her essay "Social Factors in Architecture, 1960–2004" provides a good summary of the early work on human-centered design and its integration into the Berkeley curriculum for a period that lasted into the late early 1980s. "In the 1960s in Berkeley and across the US, challenge and change were the order of the day. The gap between the perceptions and values of those who were planning and designing our cities and buildings, and those who would ultimately live in the environments created, came to the fore . . . . across the country this 'gap' began to be hotly debated by a diverse group of professionals across a wide range of disciplines."[14]

Yet almost half a century later, the gap between social science research related to designed environments and design practice remains huge, apparently because the social scientist's interest in evidence-based design leads designers to fear their creativity may be stifled.

To be empathic, design must be human centered—it must consider the needs of the end user, including physical and emotional health, and the connection to others and nature. Equal consideration must be given to the end user regardless of economic status, race, or class.

It is often people without means who are affected negatively by our built environment to a greater extent. They are often left with fewer options for healthy housing, with limited access to transit, options for walking, and green space.

The effect of the built environment on human health has gained attention from the perspective of indoor air quality in buildings (ventilation as well as toxicity of materials), access to natural sunlight and other natural elements (biophilic design), potential for community interaction (emotional health and community resilience), and opportunities to walk, bike, and take transit (lowering obesity rates, emotional health). While research and information sources supporting these topics have increased, significant opportunities remain for designers to consider these human-centered aspects. While the green-building movement is changing the way we think about healthy buildings, a lack of common sense or consideration of expenses over the health of the end user is still prevalent. Some early work on human-centered design provides valuable lessons for moving toward empathic design.

While post-occupancy evaluation developed good information on the social use of space, there was little knowledge or study of human health as affected by designed space. The first studies began in Germany in the 1950s and 1960s as the country was being rebuilt after World War II. During the war, petrochemical-based science grew enormously, and in the post-war era, these chemicals found their way into new building materials. The term *Bau-Biologie* ("Biological Building") was coined by Dr. Hubert Palm, a medical doctor, in Germany in the 1960s. He was one of the first to observe the declining health of the population as a direct result of living in housing built after World War II using the new "chemically enhanced" technologies.

A group of concerned professionals, including Palm, Dr. Anton Schneider, and Wolfgang Maes, determined that the building materials in the new buildings contained VOCs (volatile organic compounds) that had not off-gassed. As people were getting sick in the new buildings only, they began looking at the qualities of the older, prewar buildings and the outcome was a science-based exploration of the relationship between human health and building. Schneider founded a working group on "Healthy Building and Living" in 1969 in Germany, followed by the Institut für Baubiologie und Ökologie in Neubeuern, Germany, in 1976.

The institute has developed twenty-five principles of building health—these include building with natural materials, minimizing electrical fields, and considering harmonic proportion in design. Buildings can be seen as a third "skin" which interacts with the natural world and facilitates a balanced exchange of air and humidity.

Architect Helmut Ziehe founded the International Institute for Bau-Biologie® and Ecology (IBE) first in England, bringing it to the United States in 1987. Much of Bau-Biologie's focus has been on the detrimental health effects of electromagnetic radiation, or EMR. It is the only organization that has set health standards for EMRs and trained people to measure for them. (Ziehe

Garden—Villa Serbelloni

was recently honored for his work in the field of health and environment at the 25th IBE anniversary as the recipient of the 2012 Environmental Hall of Fame Lifetime Achievement Award.)

A US leader in the field is architect Paula Baker-Laporte, who became interested in healthy buildings because she suffered from chemical sensitivities. She suggests that human health issues have been overlooked by building product manufacturers for the same reason that the food industry often produces unhealthy food products. In ignoring the potential health effects of these lifeless engineered consumables, Baker-Laporte believes we've gone down the same road with our housing and health. "People don't know until they get sick that housing can actually make them sick . . . . we have created a building paradigm that does not support health or longevity of the building. The products that we put into homes are still, in large part, a spin-off from the post-war 'Better Living Through Chemistry' credo. . . . It's time for 'green' to embrace human health as well as energy efficiency and create buildings that are healthy for the environment and the occupants so that one seamlessly nurtures the other . . . . the difficulty is that 'green' is industry based, so it would be like telling General Mills to take on human health. We need a societal paradigm shift, rather than an industry-led incremental improvement of the status quo."[15]

Until the 1960s, ventilation in homes occurred naturally. Homes were "loosely built," allowing enough outside air to flow through the home to keep the air quality healthy. Prior to the energy crisis of 1973, the average home averaged approximately one air exchange per hour. Now, in a well-sealed home, the air is only exchanged once every five hours, which is not enough for optimal health.[16] With the oil embargo of 1973, insulating and sealing homes became a priority. Tighter, more energy efficient buildings trap chemicals, reducing air exchange, and the reduction of outdoor-indoor exchange tends to concentrate particles, gases, and chemicals that can lead to more chemical exposures.[17]

To make matters worse, the synthetic building materials used to seal out air and water often result in the trapping and condensation of water vapors in the walls, leading to mold and deterioration.[18] Baker-Laporte points out that much of the mass-produced building materials used today, such as paper-backed dry wall, pressed board, and carpeting, serve as "mold food." There has been a simultaneous rise in overall levels of indoor mold with this airtight method of construction. Mold can affect the nervous system, respiratory system, and suppress the immune system. However, mold cannot live in a house that is properly ventilated. Homes used to be built of natural, nonpolluting materials. In recent years, indoor air has become at least five to ten times more polluted than outdoor air and is often too polluted for optimal health. "Historically, regional building types throughout the world evolved over time as local materials were fashioned into a perfect response for the surrounding climactic conditions. Now, our homes are constructed the same regardless of location, climate, etc. Not only is this bad for the environment, it is bad for us."[19]

Building-related illness has arisen as a new phenomenon in the past thirty-five years. Exposure to toxins in the indoor environment has been linked to a wide range of illnesses, including chronic sinus infections, headaches, insomnia, anxiety, multiple chemical sensitivity, and other immune system disorders.[20] There has also been a 70 percent increase in childhood asthma over the last twenty years.[21] Americans today spend more than 90 percent of their time indoors, and indoor air pollution is one of the top four environmental health risks identified by the EPA and the scientific advisory board authorized by Congress to consult with the EPA on technical matters.[22]

My first experience with the issue of human-centered design research occurred in the 1950s on my first job after graduating architecture school—working for a San Francisco firm that specialized in school design. The boomer generation of kids was going to school and new schools were being built everywhere. I was working on drawings for a school in San Mateo, just south of San Francisco. The only windows in each of the thirty-by-thirty-foot classrooms were two vertical floor-to-ceiling strips eighteen inches wide located at the front and back of the only wall facing outdoors.

I asked the head of the design firm, who had taught many years at MIT, why there weren't more windows? He told me of a study done in window-wall and almost windowless classrooms in which a movie camera recorded the entire day. The team then counted the number of times children turned their head to look at the outside wall rather than facing forward toward the teacher. In the window-wall classroom, students often had their heads swiveled toward the outdoors. In the window-deprived classroom, seldom did they stare at the blank wall. The conclusion was that those students facing forward were paying attention to the teacher, those looking out the window were not. The "research" had been used to sell school districts on windowless classrooms and high-level artificial lighting.

I was reminded of the work of Frank and Lillian Gilbreth in the early 1900s, which used the new technology of the motion picture camera to film workers in manufacturing plants, to improve worker efficiency through detailed analysis of their performance captured in time and movement. The Gilbreths, along with Frederick Taylor, were founders of "scientific management" and their work was probably a model for the windowless classroom research; however, the methodology and the conclusions were not science. "Head forward" is not a measure of whether a student is paying attention. The students were not interviewed about their experience in the classroom and their performance was not considered. Subsequent studies showed that windowless classrooms actually depressed student performance, while similar studies in hospitals by Roslyn Lindeim and Roger Barker of the Midwest Psychological Field Station at the University of Kansas, showed that patients recovered faster when they had a view to the outside, particularly of natural environments.[23]

Since much of the healthy building research originated in Europe, and only in the last fifteen years has had a visible presence in the United States, building codes have yet to update their health and safety regulations to reflect current scientific data on healthy building and also global climate change. The building products manufacturers and the construction and real estate industries have a great financial and legal interest what is in and what is *not* in building code requirements. One glaring issue in recent years has been the use of Chinese manufactured sheetrock, which has been proved to be toxic and responsible for many health problems but has been used in constructing 65,000 homes. While the USGBC LEED building rating systems has been adopted by many federal, state, and local agencies, the American Chemistry Council, which represents the chemical, oil, and plastics industry and is a powerful lobby in Washington, refuses to work with USGBC on research or regulation regarding chemical impacts on humans. Gail Vittori, a former board chair of USGBC and a human health activist for thirty years, also finds that the medical profession has a very minimal understanding of chemical-induced illnesses. But through the empathic work of health and design activists, human health and well-being are finding their way back into the design equation.

A promising development in green-building rating systems is the cutting-edge Living Building Challenge (LBC). Developed initially by Jason F. McLennan and Bob Berkebile of BNIM Architects, it is the centerpiece of the International Living Future Institute and the Cascadia Green Building Council, led by McLennan. Its vision includes buildings that at a minimum are "triple net zero (water, energy, waste)." Its other "petals" design criteria include site, materials, human health, social equity, and beauty. The last criteria—beauty—is a stunner in a profession that has buried the term. LBC is not based on design assumptions like LEED, but on actual performance after completion.

So far, only four Living Buildings have been certified, yet nearly 150 other projects are in various stages of design in several countries around the world. One of the more notable emerging projects is the Bullitt Center Building in Seattle, which was recently completed. This six-story, 50,000-square-foot building has its top five stories framed in sustainably harvested timber, in addition to producing all its own energy from the sun and receiving all its water from rainwater. It also has composting toilets and has banned fourteen toxic chemicals from use in any of its construction materials, including phthalates, which are known immune system disrupters used in many building products. The project also required changing some of Seattle's building code regulations with the cooperation of Seattle's Department of Planning and Development. The project and the Living Building Challenge are examples of where we can go with vision and leadership from the profession, the building industry, government, and smart clients.

Today, more and more forward-thinking companies are wisely considering how their employees are using space. For example, a recent article in *Vanity Fair* by architectural critic Paul Goldberger on Google's new campus in California notes, "What is really striking about this project, however, isn't what the architecture will look like, about which renderings can show only so much anyway. It's the way in which Google decided what it wanted and how it conveyed this to its architects. Google is, as just about everyone in the world now knows, the most voracious accumulator of data on the planet. When it decided to build a building, it did what it did best, which was to gather data. Google studied, and tried to quantify, everything about how its employees work, about what kind of spaces they wanted, about how much it mattered for certain groups to be near certain other groups, and so forth."[24]

The layout of bent rectangles, then, emerged out of the company's insistence on a floor plan that would maximize "casual collisions of the work force." No employee in the 1.1-million-square-foot complex will be more than a two-and-a-half-minute walk from any other. David Radcliffe, a civil engineer who oversees Google's real estate, said, "You can't schedule innovation. We want to create opportunities for people to have ideas and be able to turn to others right there and say, 'What do you think of this?'"[25] A lot of this seems like a statement of the obvious, but then again, lots of data is. And architecture, which is so often form-driven, doesn't necessarily suffer from a bit more attention to factors other than shapes. "We started not with an architectural vision but with a vision of the work experience," Radcliffe said. "And so we designed this from the inside out."[26]

Hill Town—Italy

3 | Nature-Centered Design

Nature holds the key to our aesthetic, intellectual, cognitive and even spiritual satisfaction.

—*E. O. Wilson*

NATURE CAN LIVE WITHOUT HUMANS, but humans cannot live without nature. Architecture can make this truth transparent and allow us to experience nature at a deep, transformative level. An important mission of green building and sustainable design is to bring architecture and urban planning back into the flow and cycles of nature. We need to reconnect buildings to their roots in climate, land, and place for current and future generations. We need to design with the understanding of our genetic need to be connected to living natural environments (biophilia).[1] Architects need to not only reduce the obscene, mindless consumption and waste in the name of design, but design regenerative, living systems. We can make buildings and communities whole through commonsense design that incorporates life-enhancing technologies that incorporate the basic elements of sun, water, healthy landscapes, and clean air wherever possible.

How can design truly reflect the beauty, intimacy, complexity, and dynamic qualities of the living world?

The terms *sustainability* and *green* describe technical fixes to what are basically unsustainable systems. They can slow the rate at which things get worse, but they can't take us to a truly sustainable and healthy world. They can increase material and energetic efficiency, but they fail to radically restructure the predominantly suburban living pattern we've been building for seventy-five years—single-family-home suburbs linked by massive highways and energy grids and single-occupancy vehicles driving every day to offices, industrial malls, and central cities. Even if suburban houses are green and cars are fuel efficient, it is like greening the *Titanic* by having deck chairs made of certified wood and hemp covers. The carbon footprint of the typical suburban commuter is two to four times greater than an urban household living in multi-family dwellings and using public transportation.

I find the term *regenerative* useful because it suggests the self-healing, self-organizing, and self-evolving properties of living systems, which can coevolve with design and designers grounded in natural systems logic, or "eco-logic." For purposes of this chapter, I use the term *ecological design*.

Let's consider ecology and design. Let's consider everything that humans design as "infrastructure." That includes all buildings and services such as roads, communications, energy, sewer and water lines, and all technologies that alter the given world of nature such as genetic engineering, agriculture, industrial processes, wars, and resource extraction. What I call "ecostructure" is the design of the planet evolved over four billion years: the biosphere, its ecosystems, and all the cycles, flows, and feedback processes that make it all work together. Our real work as designers is to bring infrastructure and ecostructure together by designing infrastructure that mimics and replicates how the natural world works.

For example, we spend billions to design and build sewage treatment plants that remove organic matter from what was potable water. A marsh serves the same function ecologically. We should design sewage systems that restore wetlands, reducing flooding as well as naturally purifying wastewater at a cost far lower than the mechanical-chemical treatment plants we are still building. If we think of buildings as organisms rather than objects, then we design buildings that generate their own energy from the sun, reprocess their wastes on-site, collect and reuse rainwater, and use plant materials on roofs and walls to absorb carbon, produce oxygen, and also grow edible plants.

These connections were being made by designers in the 1960s and 1970s. The social change movement of the sixties fueled an interest in how design practices could be improved to better serve the inhabitants of designed environments. In the case of nature-centered design, interest was sparked by the seventies' focus on new forms of culture and environment. The Lindisfarne Association, founded in 1972 by cultural historian William Irwin Thompson and funded by Laurence Rockefeller and other philanthropists, became for me, and thirty-five other members who met each year for a week of formal and informal discussion, a rich and diverse source of ideas feeding into concepts of nature-centered design. I've attended these annual meetings for more than thirty years. Much of what I learned in this rich soup of empathy and knowledge has informed my approach to how living systems can be incorporated into architecture and design.

The visionary Paolo Soleri and I were the two architects in the group. The truly deep thinkers included anthropologist Gregory Bateson, atmospheric scientist James Lovelock, and microbiologist Lynn Margulis, co-authors of the "Gaia hypothesis," economist E. F. Schumacher, and biologist John Todd, who invented biological waste treatment systems using plants and fish to replace mechanical and chemical treatment of sewage waters. John was also the first person I heard using the term *ecological design* in the 1980s. Paul Mankiewicz, another biologist and founder of the Gaia Institute in New York City, for forty years has designed and built many significant projects that demonstrate how human communities and natural systems can coexist and create benefits for each. Plant breeder Wes Jackson has spent a lifetime developing perennial wheat, which reduces the erosion and destruction of soil and water when annual crops are mechanically harvested.

Sawtooth Mountains—Idaho

Wendell Berry, a farmer and poet, has been a strong voice for honoring the culture of local agriculture as the key to a healthy and stable society and environment.

The fruits of many of the ideas shared at the Lindisfarne meetings and other conferences and projects were distilled in the 1996 book I authored with Stuart Cowan, *Ecological Design.* The book outlines five basic principles of ecological design:

1. The best design solutions start with paying attention to the unique qualities of site and place.
2. Trace the direct and indirect costs to living systems of a designed project. This is far more difficult than it might seem. Many building products manufacturers are unwilling to share their data. The impacts of actions that alter ecosystems are most often not easily measurable and quantifiable.
3. Mimic nature's processes so your designs fit nature. This almost always requires adding specialists—ecologists, biologists, and others with special knowledge of natural systems, to the design team, as well as users themselves. As discussed in chapter 2, I seldom see students who can make design connections to nature.

4. Honor every voice in the design process—especially those who will live and work in your building.

5. Make nature visible through design, which will transform both designer and users.[2]

I've always been a big believer in, whenever possible, designing a site and building so that users and visitors learn something about the sacred five elements of sun, water, soil, wind, and space. The Real Goods Solar Living Center, located several hours' drive north of San Francisco, takes this idea quite far. Completed in 1996, the Center is a 5,000-square-foot building that serves as the showroom for Real Goods Trading Company and a learning center for sustainable living practices. The site is on a stream that had been destroyed by gravel mining, and I convinced the company that before starting construction they needed to spend a year restoring the site through stabilizing the damaged stream, building ponds, and planting trees. Together with a local landscape company we planted many fruit trees and dug two shallow ponds, which serve as an aesthetic feature and to store runoff on-site. As visitors approach the building, they see a large recycled redwood water tank, the start of the water story. The water flows into a biodynamic flow form and from there into a child's playground and from there through a series of channels, winding up in the ponds. The water is pumped with a solar pump, and I would watch to see people's reactions as clouds came in and the water flow quieted. The solar story is particularly important because a major part of the Real Goods business is solar electricity. I designed a series of spectrum prisms in the entranceway, facing directly south, creating a solar clock, with noon directly south. Whenever possible, recycled materials were used in the construction. The space was so well daylighted that the store's lights never come on until dark. Most unusual are the bathrooms, which we tiled in recycled toilet lids hauled from local dumps. Urine and feces are not diluted with water, but are composted on-site, another aspect of the water and regeneration story. I've studied visitors' reactions there on many occasions. I loved each time that I saw someone make a connection between the site and building design and its interaction with nature's design.

Ecological architecture is a dynamic adaptation to three key elements: people, place, and metabolism. In chapter 2, we discussed the need to design with the actual users of a completed design in the front of our minds. An ecological building is designed

Moon over Sausalito

to adapt to changing human needs and wants while meeting the needs of natural systems.

That brings us to place. "Place" implies all those ecological connections, flows, cycles, webs, and networks—cultural as well as physical—that give a place its character and qualities. While all this seems rather obvious, in the era of a global worldview that highlights the values of Westernized progress and consumption, as well as the "virtual world," place is dematerialized. As James Kunstler writes in *The Geography of Nowhere*, "we are disregarding the physical and cultural context that makes one place unique from another."[3]

Ecologists study the natural systems of a particular place by tracing all the energy and material input and output flows through the organism or system: its metabolism. Thinking about designed systems as analogous to living systems in metabolic terms is critical in our world where the consequences to living systems that result from the built environments we create are enormous.

Take the typical home as an example. Before the home was built, its site may have been a forest, grassland, farmland, or wetland, each with its own metabolic flows converting solar energy to biomass, absorbing carbon dioxide, producing oxygen, and providing habitat for a myriad of small creatures, each with their own metabolic cycles. All these cycles are altered by the act of building. To construct the house, trees are cut in far-off locations, metals refined, plastics manufactured. When the house is completed, a new set of cycles comes into play. Gas, oil, or electricity is burned to heat, cool, and light the house. The output of carbon dioxide and waste heat is dumped into the atmosphere. The occupants burn fuel in order to travel from and to the house. Food grown in far-off locations is purchased and consumed, and the wastes disposed in landfills. Clean water is piped in and discharged together with human wastes and other debris.

Multiply the single home by tens of millions. We find the metabolic flows arising from human design decisions and living patterns have a huge impact on the metabolism of human systems at a planetary scale. The whole process involves complex economic, industrial, governmental, and cultural ecologies that have yet to be mapped. We are still in the first stages of translating ecological thinking into design tools that allow us to trace metabolic effects through the system. Today there are not many incentives for doing so, since government regulations and our economic system tend to ignore the impact of self-interest upon the common interest, and the relationship among the three types of capital: financial, human, and natural.

The British architect Frank Duffy first noted an important insight regarding architecture and the layering of its pulse, or metabolism. Modern buildings are composed of five major layered systems—site, structure, services, skin, and stuff—each having a progressively more rapid life cycle and metabolic rates. Their different pulses are affected by technological and cultural change (new fashions and inventions), the effects of environment and weather (oxidation and UV exposure), and geotechnical and ecosystem effects (earthquake, floods, decline and renewal of urban districts). Site presumably changes only in geologic time, although its cultural and ecological context may change so much that the site indeed becomes another site in every way except spatially.

The layers wear out at different rates. Site has the slowest metabolism. Next is structure, which generally has a life as long as that of the building. Systems such as mechanical heating and cooling have a more rapid metabolism due to parts wearing out or systems becoming obsolete. A building skin has an even shorter metabolism due to weather and wear or obsolescence. The shortest metabolism is that of stuff—movable furnishings and equipment that are regularly replaced.

Building metabolism brings into focus the question of durability and life cycle cost. Before the modern era, buildings tended to be "single layer," that is, structure, systems, and skin were one and the same. Durability was a function of the material properties of the single layer. Today, buildings are composites of different systems with different pulses and different useful lives. What is the role of durability? How do designers minimize the metabolic rate or pulse of the building as a whole or learn how to recycle metabolic processes such as waste heats?

When we begin to design buildings from the point of view of metabolism and pulse, we move to three important strategies: integrated life cycle costing, decarbonization, and dematerialization. Integrated *life-cycle costing* establishes the value of the building over time both as a whole and for its particular components. Replacing moveable furnishings does not seriously interrupt a building's use, whereas replacing an HVAC system does. Integrating mechanical systems with natural systems—such as daylighting plus artificial light, or natural ventilation plus mechanical ventilation—are strategies to introduce redundancy into our buildings, extending useful life, and reducing metabolism.

Reducing the flow of carbon in buildings is critical to coping with global warming and climate chaos. The obvious measures include energy efficiency and climate responsive design. The latter, if taken seriously, would outlaw our current "big box" building footprints that cannot function without massive energy-intensive HVAC and lighting systems. Less obvious and more intriguing is to design buildings with built-in carbon sinks such as a second skin of living materials that absorb carbon dioxide and other toxins. As thirty- and forty-year-old glass and metal walls wear out, they can be replaced with a double skin of carbon dioxide absorbing plants. As parts of the urban fabric wear out, they could be replaced with forests. *Decarbonizing* strategies such as these would give true meaning to "greening the city."

Dematerialization, doing more with less by substituting design intelligence for brute force and more stuff, can easily be understood if we look at Stephen Ambrose's book *Undaunted Courage*, an account of Lewis and Clark's expedition to map the continent west of the Mississippi in 1803. Ambrose writes of the thousands of pounds of equipment required by the explorers to

Winter Ocean—Pt. Reyes, California

simply locate latitude and longitude, something we now can do with a handheld GPS. Messages to Washington, the nation's capital, had to be carried by horseback and took weeks. Per unit computing power has fallen from tons per gigabyte of information to today's microchip circuits that weigh less than an ounce. These are impressive examples of dematerialization and miniaturization through design.

As ecological designer Josiah Raison Cain explains,

> *Nature centered design can bring an elemental awareness of natural processes and interactions into even the urban context. Reflected light of cities hides the night sky, underground drains hide water courses, and distant landfills hide cycles of biological decay and renewal. The challenge is to make long-hidden natural processes both visible and viable. We can make transparent the processes by which humanity procures food, air, water, and other things essential to survival. What we may learn is that the things we love are also the things that maintain a healthy environment in which to live; we can embrace a healthy natural world as an important part of*

engineering our living environments. We will learn that an important part of "design intuition" is our inherent ability to recognize healthy ecosystems as "beautiful" and design a world around us that is inclusive.

It is within our grasp to dramatically reduce the resource demands and waste flows of urban systems by understanding and incorporating natural systems and processes. This includes regional green infrastructure systems, more localized "eco-districts," and building scale innovation. There is a great likelihood that these solutions combined with renewable energy, smart grid, and other technological applications can bring the impact of human activity within a manageable range. It is worth noting that both San Francisco and Vancouver satisfied Kyoto Protocols within the past few years. The economic and cultural vitality of these cities demonstrates that green is not necessarily lean. To the contrary, efforts to meet Kyoto in both cities have stimulated innovation and sustainable business, creating jobs and regional affluence.

The earth's epidermis is essentially a living skin, proportionally thinner than the shell of an egg, inhabited by approximately 10 million diverse species. All known life lives within this fragile but resilient lens. We are most familiar with a soil layer of about 6' and the associated vegetation that is home to most terrestrial biology, and the oceans. The function of this "skin" includes the production of oxygen, capture and conversion of solar energy, carbon sequestration, food production, temperature modulation, erosion control, soil production, air filtration, pathogen control, and the distillation, filtration, and redistribution of freshwater resources, to name a few. From a sustainability and life support systems standpoint, it is wildly productive.

Skin is also a term commonly used to describe the outer surface of a building. These glass, wood, and concrete surfaces are hard, slippery, and inhospitable to life. Air pollutants cling to inert surfaces and scarcely degrade. Water rushes in a torrent with nothing to slow or sink it, and so it gathers erosive speed, collecting toxins en route to the nearest pipe. In contrast to the earth's skin, we have created a new geomorphology that is wildly unproductive.

It is interesting to consider the effect of stretching the earth's epidermis over our buildings, cladding structures with living vibrant ecology. Perhaps this could provide some of the resources we import from without, including food. Certainly it would filter air and create oxygen, provide habitat, control stormwater, cool the city, and reduce the energy cost of cooling the buildings themselves. Research is suggesting it would have a beneficial effect on the psychology of the inhabitants as well, improving creativity, health, focus, and mood.

Ecological design borrows from biological systems by observation. Nature combats instability in a particular environment by evolving an integrated or linked diversity in which many species at all scales are connected through flows and cycles. Rivers are designed to flood without doing harm. Their banks are lined with trees that prevent erosion. Their immediate low-lying areas, or floodplains, are populated with plants and animals that are adapted to thrive on occasional floods. Those places where two kinds of natural systems come together—for example, where forest meets grassland or where tidal waters meet land—are called "ecotones," and they are typically places of maximum biological diversity and productivity. They are constantly changing, yet maintain relative stability. We can apply the same thinking in designing the future of our cities and regions.

Our future is in nature. Designers have amassed quite a toolkit for deep sustainability. Solutions generally do not survive if they are not cost effective. The last decade has provided a testing ground for innovation. Markets have matured, and new industries are emerging around greywater and rainwater, vegetated architectural systems, renewable energy, clean tech, urban agriculture, green materials, and professional services.

What becomes clear is that separation from nature has deprived us of not only experiential but also functional benefits. We have come to rely too heavily upon the mechanical world and cannot imagine how we survive without it. In this time of uncertainty we have the option to embrace the natural world and save it simply by encouraging it to thrive around us.[4]

In 2005, I was one of two dozen leaders in the green building field who met at the Rockefeller Conference Center in the Pocantico Hills outside New York City to share their views on an expanding approach to green, having reached consensus that improving our technological fixes, such as LEED, are not sufficient to meet the magnitude of change needed to sustain, restore, and regenerate our communities and planet. Seven common needs emerged from the discussion that were relevant to the work I was doing in the 1960s and 1970s and are still relevant today.

1. Move away from a totally human-centered view of the world.
2. Understand the synergy between nature and human nature.
3. Appreciate the interconnectedness of the whole.
4. Use principles of living systems in our work as architects and ecological designers.
5. See ourselves as continual learners and avoid hubris.

6. Encourage dialogue and ask deeper questions, especially when challenging accepted ways of thinking and doing.
7. Recognize the role of spirit and love in everything we do.

My hope is that as society increasingly acknowledges the critical value to our health and well-being through a direct connection to nature, designing with nature will become a major tool toward creating a vital new architecture for an empathic world.

Villa—Italy

4 | Lifetime Learning Design

*I have never let my schooling interfere with my
education.*

—*Mark Twain*

FORMAL ARCHITECTURAL EDUCATION STARTED IN TWO TYPES
OF INSTITUTIONS in Europe in the late nineteenth century.
The polytechnic institutes in France and Germany focused on
engineering and sciences; the art schools, such as the École des
Beaux-Arts in France, focused on individual artistic ability in
drawing, painting, and design. The latter became the model for

most architectural programs. The establishment of academic architecture programs is related to the rapid growth of the Industrial Revolution, with a widening of a wealthy merchant class, new technologies, and new building types such as factories, schools, and hospitals. There was a shift from the geometric designer/master builder handicraft in the medieval and Renaissance building to the engineer/institute-trained architect working with mechanical production of component parts and building systems.

Formal university education of architecture in the United States leading to a professional degree and licensing of architects by government began in the late nineteenth century, and today several hundred schools are accredited to offer the professional degree in architecture, usually through a two- or three-year graduate program. The primary core pedagogy in teaching architecture is the design studio, where each semester a class of fifteen to twenty-five students is assigned a design project by a teacher who has an architecture degree, but most likely limited practical experience in the field. The core of the program, the design studio in which students are given imaginary projects, omits most of the real conditions a designer would face on a real project, such as a real client, and the other members of the design/building team, such as engineers and other consultants, contractors, permitting agencies, and cost estimators. Students are given a description of the project, usually including a specific site, scope and size of the project and potential use, and general desired goals and outcomes. Each student works alone two to four months on the project, developing floor plans, elevations, sections, and perspective drawings. Until the modern computer age, all drawings were done by hand, but today most are created using computer drawings, and many students today have no hand drawing or sketching skills. As the studio progresses, the class work is reviewed in a group review by the instructor and suggestions made. The final judging of individual work takes place through a "jury" of instructors. It is not unusual for competing students to spend numerous "all-nighters" finishing up their projects before the jury. They often arrive for the jury exhausted and unfocused. The jury members are often more interested in impressing their peers with their clever deprecating comments than in providing positive advice.

Rob Fleming distinguishes between the Competitive Design Studio model, which is still the predominant format in US schools, and Integrative Design Studios that are slowly being adopted in some schools. He writes, "The hurdle of the competitive design studio as an inhibitor to cooperative learning environments must be jumped. . . . Studio education should not be based on a concept of winning or losing, but instead on a process of learning . . . the current studio teaching methodology is focused more on product than process. . . . Professors take pride in the ability of their students to endure the punishing work load, all-nighters and caffeine induced states of reality."[1]

From a practical professional perspective, the design studio makes very little sense. Architecture is a collaborative discipline that engages architectural teams with clients, consultants, engineers, builders and developers, and numerous government agencies. Within most architecture schools, there are experts in energy efficiency, ecological design, and other related disciplines, but they are seldom consulted by the "studio masters," and their expertise is often segregated from the core design program. Each student is competing with the others, rather than collaborating, in a social Darwinian test of "creativity"—a most elusive goal. I hear over and over again that the graduates of such programs have trouble adjusting to work in architectural offices because of their lack of experience in working collaboratively, and their lack of experience in the realities of design and construction. Basically, design studios are nonempathic exercises in which you're told, "Wake up screaming in the middle of the night with a creative idea, and then find someone who wants your brilliant design." It's as though Ayn Rand thought up the concept of the brilliant loner design studio student in *The Fountainhead*.

In 1989, Clare Cooper Marcus, a colleague at Berkeley, wrote a memo to the architecture faculty noting, "Attending a number of studio reviews at the end of last semester, we became deeply disturbed at the seemingly single minded focus on appearance, and an almost total dismissal of how form might support and facilitate people's day to day needs and comfort. Of course architecture is about exploring appearance and form. . . . Our concern is that it seems to be the exclusive focus of every studio. . . . We may be in an Ivory Tower, but do we need to be socially irresponsible?"

Writing about the British architectural establishment in the *British Architectural Review*, Patrik Schumacher asks, "Should we not expect the best students and teachers at the best architecture schools to make a serious contribution to the innovative upgrading of the discipline's capacity to take on the challenges it might actually face via its future clients and commissions?"[2]

Venice, 1958

It's time to retire this 150-year-old obsolete, nonempathic, noncollaborative pedagogy. We can and must do better if architecture and architects are going to address present and future realities.

Good designers are not born that way. Most develop their talents over a lifetime of learning in many settings, often starting at an early age. When my three children went to our local Berkeley elementary schools, I made contact with their teachers who were interested in changing their classroom from the then-typical layout of fixed seats facing forward to the teacher at front of the room, to more flexible and cozier small group arrangements. My design studio class worked with teachers and their students to design and build movable interior space dividers, desks made of recycled cardboard barrels, boxes stacked as bookcase and cubby partitions. The major design material was recycled cardboard appliance boxes. The kids did much of the assembly and arrangement with our help. The whole idea was to break out of the classroom box, and for the students and teachers to design and set up the room arrangements that worked for them. We also used the design/build process to teach kids geometry, and they made large models of various geometric shapes. Over a three-year period, we worked indoors and outdoors designing and building with elementary school students and their teachers in a number of California communities.

As a child I learned to create forms with clay and also spent a lot of time drawing. At the High School of Music and Art in Manhattan, I was an art major, spending every afternoon in art class and, in my junior year, an architecture class. During the summer I worked on New England farms renovating buildings. I also worked as an assistant to the superintendent of a large-tract housing project on Long Island before going to architecture school. These experiences positively influenced the direction I took when I began teaching.

Every semester I taught a design studio with a very different form and content than the standard model described above. We focused on real projects, worked collaboratively, both designed and often built what we designed, worked with real client groups, and often worked away from campus. I always followed the adage, "teach what you most want to learn." I structured my design studios to work on improving real-life design situations.

The first Earth Day, organized by college students in the spring of 1970, during which 18 million people participated in live events, marked the flowering of the environmental movement into a major force. The movement encouraged me to begin a series of experimental design studios that would take architecture classes and students out of the classroom and into the world of diverse communities and the natural world outside the campus walls. Real situations where students could design, build, live with, and evaluate the results of their work. Before joining the Brown administration in 1975 as California State Architect and director of the Governor's Office of Appropriate Technology, I initiated a number of experimental projects that linked design to real people and natural systems through designing, building, and testing what we had designed and built. I was also inspired by a spontaneous event in the spring of 1969 where students and local residents started to rebuild a vacant plot of university land as a park. The People's Park was a grand collective design experiment bypassing the campus elite and California's new governor, Ronald Reagan.

Berkeley in the early months of 1969 was wrapped in the glory of a warm, clear spring. The vibrant town buzzed with the bustle of student activity, the thrum of political protests against the war in Vietnam. A block off Telegraph Avenue lay a festering eyesore: two square blocks of neglected land, a muddy pit of tire ruts brimming with soured spring rain. It was an irritating reminder to the neighborhood of a university plan and process gone wrong. Several years earlier, community residents and the Campus Committee on Housing & Environment, which I chaired, had risen in protest as the university tore down a lovely slice of town to make room for what the chancellor's office said would be a blockbuster medical center, although our research showed that to be untrue. They bulldozed the intricate fabric of old houses and shops that framed one side of campus. Then they let the land lie fallow. People started using it as a parking lot.

In a Telegraph Avenue coffee shop, an idea sprang up among a group of locals. "Why not turn that vacant lot into a park? Lots of people are showing up in Berkeley, hanging out, sleeping on the street. They need a nice green place to be." The idea was like a dandelion that scattered its seeds in every direction. A few days later, after coaxing donations from local merchants, a small army assembled in the vacant lot, armed with shovels and wheelbarrows. They had no plan as they started to dig. Within the following weeks, more and more people joined the effort. The common cause united folks of all stripes—students, street people, local residents with their children. It was a magical thing that captured the spirit of the time. Every evening, the workers would gather around a campfire for an informal potluck and a group meeting to decide on an ever changing plan.

"Let's dig a pool! That would be cool!" someone would say one night. The next morning would see dirt flying from a widening hole. That night from the edge of the pond-to-be, another voice would tug things in another direction: "It might be dangerous. Small kids could fall in and drown." Heads would nod and the dirt would fly right back into the hole. The collaborative design process had no single leader, and so the project seemed to wander with a life of its own. Inevitably some good ideas arose from the mass input, including that every voice should be heard because everyone could be a designer. I would often stop by on my way home from campus to observe the process. Within a few weeks, a park began to take shape. Hundreds of people laid sod, built walls of rubble concrete, laid out paths, crafted crude furniture of found materials. Each day ended with another open design session where decisions and revisions were made for the following day. This was the grand experiment.

I brought my students to the site to watch like a group of anthropologists studying a new tribe. I got a call from the chancellor, who was starting to hear from Governor Reagan's office. "What's going on there on our lot? I hear they call it 'People's Park.' Don't they know that's university property and they're trespassing?" I told him it seemed a positive experience in community building. They were transforming a nasty forgotten piece of land into a park built and used by the community. But more angry words railed down from Sacramento.

Late one night a vanguard of workers sealed off the park with a tall chain-link fence. Armed Alameda County sheriffs stood guard around the perimeter of the fence. Daybreak saw chaos and warfare around the campus and central Berkeley as students and street people rioted, enraged by the stealth seizure. National Guard helicopters sprayed the central campus with a new type of poison gas being tested for use in Vietnam. Students rushed to get inside, but all the doors to campus buildings had been locked by the police. Reagan called out the National Guard, who surrounded the park, armed with bayoneted rifles. Girls stuck fresh flowers in their gun barrels while the guardsmen stood motionless and expressionless.

People's Park still exists. The ideas and experience travelled to places far and wide, carried deep in the hearts of the participants.

Many, like me, left Berkeley and moved to rural areas free from the controlling hands of raw senseless power and the shock of a campus that had become a militarized zone like the nightly TV images we saw of the war in Vietnam. Freed from this, people could experiment in designing and building new forms of home and community that broke free from the culture of post-war suburbia. I continued teaching. The park experiment and experience set in motion for me a new way to think about our lives, my teaching and practice.

After People's Park, my family and I left Berkeley and moved into a small cabin in a coastal forest on the Northern California coast. I had taken a leave from the university and had received a Guggenheim grant to put together a book about our classroom building experiences.[3] During the late sixties I had also visited and studied a number of intentional communities in the West through a grant from the National Institute for Mental Health to a new nonprofit I had created, Community for Environmental Change. Now, away from all the chaos in Berkeley, I had time to reflect on what was next. People's Park and many of the communes I had visited were spontaneous experiments in new forms of living. I began to imagine developing integrated design learning experiences, "thought experiments," which would allow us to test design ideas through creating them and living with them. In 1971, I purchased a five-acre parcel of wilderness forest and proposed a four-day-a-week class called "Making a Place in the Country." The Architecture Department accepted my proposal with the stipulation that at the end of the semester the students and I would give a public presentation about the class.

The idea was to create a living/learning experience where students would collaboratively design and build rudimentary common facilities: places to meet, cook, and eat, and a bath and toilet. Each student would design and build his or her own shelter/sleeping space. Our first task was to find some building materials. Roaming around Sonoma County, we found ten-by-twenty-foot chicken houses built about forty years earlier by a former chicken farmer. They were well built of old-growth redwood walls and roof and straight-grained fir floors. We paid twenty-five dollars for each of them, then dismantled and transported them on our flatbed truck back to our site. A student wrote, "You took care taking down what had been built so carefully—feeling good that the coops would not die—but only be transformed."

First we built an old-fashioned outhouse, and then a kitchen out of the recycled wood. Then we built a sixteen-by-twenty-four-foot structure that served as a meeting and indoor work space—the center of our community. We called it "the Ark," after the original Bernard Maybeck–designed wooden architecture building on the Berkeley campus. As the Ark took shape, each student was invited to build their own personal shelter using various reclaimed materials we had scavenged. The individual act of imagining and building simple shelter within a community evoked deep feelings. Everyone was required to keep a daily journal. Here are some excerpts:

> *The class instilled not just a fundamental knowledge of building, but a confidence to undertake projects otherwise beyond our realm. Confidence to follow a vision.*

> *How many how to's did I learn these ten weeks, embracing a spectrum from how to hammer a nail, to how to make myself happy. A spectrum coherent, flowing, and unified. I learned how to build a house in which my physical self could live and I learned how to build a consciousness in which my spiritual self could exist.*

Barn—Sonoma

We learned the importance of local knowledge and knowing place. For me and the students in the class, it was a life-changing experience. It gave me the confidence and vision to move forward with more Thought Experiments where everyone was both student and teacher.

The next thought experiment was to research, design, and build on the campus a self-sustaining model habitat integrating various life support systems using natural energy flows of the sun, wind, water, and soil. I received permission from the chancellor's office to construct the project on a site close to the College of Environmental Design. In the fall quarter, class members researched various systems, including windmills to produce electricity, solar water heating systems, recycling human waste into nutrient-rich compost, a greenhouse to grow vegetables and heat the space, and water-conserving methods. In the vast UC library systems, there were only three books that touched on any of these topics at the time. In the second quarter, each student prepared a design for the model habitat. At the end of the quarter, we collectively selected one student design to build on the campus. In the third quarter, we built the Natural Energy Pavilion on campus.

The information collected in the first quarter was put into a 150-page document called "Natural Energy Handbook."[4] Since Earth Day 1970 and an emerging back-to-the-land movement in our region, there was a growing interest in how to live lightly and not rely on large centralized systems. Word got around about the handbook. Local bookstores wanted copies, so we started printing and selling it. We banked the money we made on the book and used it to pay for the materials to build the Pavilion. The structure took shape quickly. Most of the wood for the structure came from an abandoned barn we tore down. The flat roof held a hot water solar collector we fabricated in the Architecture Department shop. A fifty-gallon drum held rainwater from the roof, which also included a small electric wind-powered generator. The structure was completed in the spring of 1973 just as the OPEC oil embargo was creating angry long lines at gas stations and people were waking up to our almost total dependence on fossil fuels to power our society. Local TV picked up the story and soon long lines of people snaked across the campus to tour the project. The students were exhilarated and exhausted.

In the next thought experiment, I wanted to expand and tune up the technologies and principles tested in the Energy Pavilion and demonstrate them in an actual house remodel that students would design and build and then live in while operating and monitoring its systems. The demonstration home would also offer public workshops and tours so people could begin to see how they could apply the same principles and technologies in their own homes. The goals included using less energy and fewer resources while integrating growing and processing food and natural energy strategies in the home and site design.

We teamed up with UC Berkeley's College of Natural Resources. We created the nonprofit Farallones Institute, which purchased for $8,000 an old vacant house in the Berkeley flats where the rich alluvial soil washing down from the hills provided great soil for growing. We called the project "Integral Urban House." We learned that the integration of diverse disciplines—architecture and natural resource management—required sharing a common language and image that transcended the narrow jargon of the individual disciplines. The builders learned that a gram of what they called "dirt" contained millions of bacteria that processed organic matter into food for plants. The biologists learned that concrete is heavy and dries fast.

The biological strategies included tearing up the concrete sidewalk along the street, covering it with mulch to provide a home for many microorganisms as well as to absorb rainwater. The garden was planted in then-novel raised beds using the French intensive method newly introduced to the United States. On the north side of the lot were pens for chickens and rabbits, grown for food and eggs and fed largely with weeds from the garden. A fishpond and beehive completed the outdoor design. The remodeled house included a composting toilet that used no water and wasn't connected to the sewer. All the composted materials were recycled into the garden soil. The remodeled house had a greenhouse on the south side for natural warming and food production. The kitchen stove ran on wood scraps.

UC students served as interns and residents with the task of operating all the systems and keeping records, primarily what the home consumed and how much of that was produced on-site. We operated the house for ten years with interns cycling though each year and participating in a continuous stream of workshops and visitor tours. In 1979, Sierra Club Books published *The Integral Urban House: Self Reliant Living in the City*, often tagged as the most complete guide to creating integral ecologic systems at the household scale.[5] In its 25th anniversary issue, *Fine Homebuilding* magazine devoted the entire issue to presenting the twenty-five most important houses built in America since the Pilgrims landed in 1620. The Integral Urban House was one of these.

While it was under construction, a former student of mine visited the Integral Urban House. He was impressed, and expressed an interest in expanding the concepts through the design and construction of a model rural learning center that would be a larger example of the ecological and natural systems we were integrating at the Integral Urban House. He offered to fund the project through his family's philanthropic foundation. After a long search, we were offered an eighty-acre site of forested rolling hills bisected by a stream and lowland meadows in Sonoma County, north of San Francisco Bay Area. The owners, who supported our concept, offered to let us use the property as we wished with an option to purchase at a future date. Sitting on the sea cliffs near my home, taking a break from planning the new rural center, I looked out into the normally foggy ocean. Suddenly the usual fog lifted and I saw the furthest western reach of the American continent—the Farallones Islands, invisible except for occasional clear moments. At that point, I named our project the Farallones Rural Center.

I met with the Sonoma County Planning Department Director and explained that we were a nonprofit educational institute whose mission was to design, teach, and build a center that would integrate energy-efficient shelter design with food and energy production, and water-conserving and waste-recycling systems. We submitted a master plan and building plans for a kitchen/dining facility, a bathhouse, and composting toilets. Students and staff would live on-site in tents until we could design and build housing.

In June 1975, we offered a two-month program called Whole Life Systems, followed by a one-year apprenticeship in solar building design and construction, farming and gardening, energy systems, ecosystems management, and community living skills. Our hands-on, experiential learning-by-doing method was unusual for college-level education. "Making a Place in the Country" had lit the vision and convinced me it could work. Out of scores of applicants, we selected twenty students with diverse backgrounds. The group decided that priorities should be developing the food garden, converting an old garage into a shop and a visitors center, and building five cabins, each with a different approach to solar design. The experiment, monitored with equipment from the local utility, was the first in the nation to compare different residential-scale solar heating and cooling techniques.

After the first summer of operation at the Rural Center, I joined Governor Jerry Brown's administration as California State Architect, overseeing all of the State design and construction, and also as director of a newly created Governor's Office of Appropriate Technology. The Rural Center continued to grow and thrive, adding many new programs and serving a wide variety of audiences. Weekend and weeklong gardening workshops teaching new organic methods and workshops in Community Technology were added. In 1979, we were awarded a major contract by the Peace Corps to intensively train volunteers in Appropriate Technology before their assignment to overseas service. Our trainers went to field locations all over the world to do follow-up training.

Paul Hawken writes in our 1979 Annual Report, "From the outset Rural Center has been concerned with creating a community of architects, scientists, biologists, builders, craftspeople and gardeners who could evolve a living system within what is being called 'Appropriate Technology.' The Rural Center devoted most of each teaching activities to hands-on pursuits, instructing how to apply appropriate technology in everyday life. The main focuses have been intensive organic agriculture, solar house design and construction, and the development of household water systems stressing greywater use and composting toilets. They are examining all aspects of daily life—in a sense taking them apart and putting them back together again."

The institute continues today as the Occidental Arts and Ecology Center. I'm grateful they have been able to continue the work and take the Rural Center's mission to whole new levels.

After five years in state government, I returned to teaching, and when I did, I continued new thought experiments, focusing on urban community projects. Over the years, I have come to feel strongly that eco-literacy—learning how to think, act, and live ecologically—and design education can and should start early in a child's life. Through our new nonprofit, the Ecological Design Institute, and with the support of the Center for Eco-Literacy, we undertook the design of K-12 school programs that integrated ecological design education with eco-literacy.

I am convinced that design cannot meet its full potential until both the general public and future professional designers start to learn design and ecology through project-based, hands-on learning early in their lives.

The hands-on design studios I've described in this chapter were an exception to the prevailing rules at the time, but over the years, more architecture programs have initiated and supported efforts similar to mine, such as Sam Mockbee's Rural Studio in Alabama where students work with poor rural families to design new homes. "The main purpose of the Rural Studio is to enable each student to step across the threshold of misconceived opinions and to design/build with a 'moral sense' of service to a community. It is my hope that the experience will help the student of architecture to be more sensitive to the power and promise of what they do, to be more concerned with the good effects of architecture than with 'good intentions.'"[6]

The Yestermorrow School in Vermont offers design/build programs designed to inspire the creation of "a better, more sustainable world by providing hands-on education that integrates design and craft as a creative, interactive process."[7] Emily Piliton's

Project H works with high school students to redesign and rebuild classrooms. The Solar Decathalon program, sponsored by the US Department of Energy since 2002, challenges collegiate architecture school teams to design, build, and operate solar homes. Since its beginning, the program has involved 112 collegiate teams affecting 17,000 participants, and the exhibit of entries over the years has attracted 350,000 visitors. The Decathalon invites academic institutions to "design, build, and operate solar-powered houses that are cost-effective, energy-efficient, and attractive. The winner of the competition is the team that best blends affordability, consumer appeal, and design excellence with optimal energy production and maximum efficiency."[8]

Habitat for Humanity and Architecture for Humanity, neither connected to a collegiate architecture program, provide design, development, and construction services in this country and worldwide. What they do, and how they work, needs to be integrated into design education, which is so insulated from the reality of how most of the world lives.

While these programs and projects provide hope for the future, systematic changes in the way architecture programs are designed are needed. The discipline of architecture needs to be approached in a more collaborative and integrated way. Jason McLennan recalls, "We were encouraged to think about these issues—and to work collaboratively with other disciplines and clients—but it was academic only, not literal. There is always an underlying focus on the architect as heroic individual solving things in isolation."[9]

Clues to the formation of new design educational processes come from Jeremy Rifkin: "Because empathic skills emphasize a nonjudgmental orientation and tolerance of other perspectives, they accustom young people to think in terms of layers of complexity and force them to live within the context of ambiguous realities where there are no simple formulas or answers, but only a constant search for shared meanings and common understandings."[10] The integrative design studio, instead of pitting students against each other, is a cooperative venture, generally selects an actual design project based in the community, and brings together community advocates and participants from many disciplines. The rich interactive process—a design workshop or charette—is based in the real world and stresses listening to all voices, presenting and analyzing many ideas and possible solutions. Design charettes are open source and transparent. Personal ownership of ideas is exchanged for achieving something much larger—an expression of a collective ideal. This allows for alignment among client, designer, engineer, and builder—a more streamlined process.

The charette is optimistic, uplifting and cooperative in spirit (when done well), and offers an avenue for educators to address the competitive nature of many design studios. It is common for design charettes to feature multiple teams working in parallel in a friendly competition to develop the best scheme in response to a given challenge. In the educational environment, the presence of multiple disciplines and the inclusion of community members can temper the competitive yearnings of young design students.

The charette builds a "transdisciplinary culture" where each discipline receives the respect it deserves through the establishment of domain expertise but also through the effective participation across scales in the design process. For example, landscape architects can begin to offer suggestions about the use of plants to purify indoor air quality or architects can make suggestions regarding a better layout of ductwork for either performance or aesthetic reasons.

Design charettes are nonhierarchical in their spatial arrangements. This reinforces a sense of equity and encourages maximum participation. Small breakout groups work closely with a faculty member, domain expert, or other assigned facilitator during work sessions. Later in the semester, students begin to lead the table as they gain comfort and skill in mediating group dynamics.

In their 1996 study of architectural education, Ernest Boyer and Lee Mitgang remind us of the need to move the evolution of design studio further and quicker: "To promote a caring climate for learning, schools of architecture must be places where students feel supported rather than hazed. An overly competitive, intimidating atmosphere takes away from this purpose. The point is that the education of architects must develop in students a sensitivity to the needs of and concerns of others from individual clients to whole communities."[11]

As with many ways forward that offer hope for the future, architecture education may want to look for inspiration in the natural world. As Tom Fisher of the University of Minnesota School of Architecture states, "It's all about creating an intellectual ecosystem as diverse and healthy as a natural one."[12]

Ocean Evening—BC Canada

5 | Opportunities for Empathic Design

*It's not about your greatness as an architect, but your
compassion.*

—Samuel Mockbee

HAVING LOOKED AT WHERE WE HAVE BEEN AND WHERE WE
ARE NOW, we take a look at where we can go with empathic
design. We can begin by making some assumptions regarding our
future and how it will affect all of us and the nature of design.
Climate chaos and global warming will reshape our institutions,
our societies, how we live, and how and what we design.

In the 1970s, atmospheric scientist James Lovelock and microbiologist Lynn Margolis were the first to propose a modern scientific perspective that saw Earth as a single, complex, cooperative living organism. At first, many scientists were skeptical of their Gaia hypothesis, but today a general consensus among scientists from many disciplines view Gaia theory as both science and metaphor—a means of understanding how we might begin addressing twenty-first-century issues such as climate change and ongoing environmental destruction.

The work of Lovelock and Margulis on the Gaia concept followed a few years after we saw the powerful image of Earth in the first photos astronauts took of our home—a delicate blue ball in endless space. The underlying impetus to design empathically is to re-create our fundamental relationship to Gaia in a way that supports her, not just us. There are many good examples of new ways people are honoring the sacred elements of sun, water, and soil, making them part of a solution to saving Gaia and ourselves. We are still dependent on these basic elements, but our modern technological culture is disconnected from them. We need to realign our use of Gaia's basic elements of energy, food, and water.

Most ironically, oil and coal—not discovered until the Industrial Revolution—were gifts from Gaia in the form of ancient decomposed organic matter from land and marine plants and animals. The continued reckless exploitation and use of fossil fuel technologies in modern society may wreck Gaia and all who live with her.

As California State Architect in the 1970s, I was highly influenced by the studies of F. King Hubbert, Chief Geologist of the US Geological Survey and a longtime oil geologist. His prediction at the time was that US oil production had peaked in the seventies and would severely decline by the turn of the century. His work motivated me and others in state government to propose changes to California's building codes, calling for a 40 percent reduction in energy use by buildings. The OPEC oil embargo, which cut off foreign oil imports to this country in 1973, was another wake-up call to our dependence on oil. To show what was possible, we designed and built in a three-year period a major new state office building that reduced energy consumption by 85 percent from the then existing standard.[1]

"Peak oil" remains an issue, although its major impact seems to have been to frighten people, or turn them into survivalists, rather than to constructively model how we might work together to create more resilient communities. In the last year, the planet's most effective advocate to reduce global warming, Bill McKibben, founder of 350.org, released data that showed that the fossil fuel companies have five times more reserves than the amount previously thought available to hold further temperature rise to two degrees Celsius, a number at the tipping point of doomsday. Fossil fuels and the carbon and other chemical pollution they produce are Mother Earth's fatal dose of cancer.

An opportunity for empathic designers to lessen the impact of climate chaos is to use renewable energy from sun and wind to replace our fossil-fuel-based energy grid. In the United States, solar and wind each supply about 1 percent of our total energy supply. A solar thermal facility covering a hundred by a hundred square miles on the Nevada test site could supply our country's total energy demand. However, there's one big problem. It would take an estimated two trillion dollars to upgrade the country's energy grid for power to flow efficiently across the country. The smart move today is to localize energy production by creating community-based solar microgrids as well as rooftop solar on homes and other buildings. The cost of solar electric panels has decreased sharply in recent years—most are now produced in China—and at today's electric rates would pay for themselves in 10 to 15 years. Germany's solar energy supplies 20 percent of its demand, showing a shift to solar and wind is doable. Government needs to provide incentives to create more local solar energy. We need a national campaign using the model of sales house parties that commercial companies like Avon and Tupperware used in the fifties to push their products door to door.

I live in a wealthy county with lots of intelligent people who want to do the right thing; yet we have very few solar-roofed homes in a community where most of the homes are one story and solar panels would be simple to install. Instead, we have a County Energy Agency advertising that it provides us with "green renewable energy," but their claim is misleading. They use our money to buy "renewable energy credits" that subsidize Shell Oil–brokered wind farms in Texas and elsewhere, while its customers receive the same electricity that all other utility customers get. No green electrons flow into our non-solar homes, while solar homes such as mine feed green electrons back into the utility grid, reducing my net electrical use from the grid.

Ward Lake—California

A better model for local energy systems that is growing rapidly in Europe and starting up in the United States is the local energy microgrid at the neighborhood, town, or community scale. The three components of the microgrid are a renewable energy generator such as rooftop solar panels or solar tracking poles, electronic controls that monitor the system and distribute energy to the connected users, and storage for surplus energy, which for solar electricity would be batteries. As electric plug-in cars begin to replace gasoline-powered vehicles, small-scale neighborhood microgrids will replace gas stations. While interest in local energy systems has increased since the power outages related to Superstorm Sandy, the systems are slow to change.

When people actually see, touch, and feel how renewable energy and other green technologies work, they experience the potential for technology that is in harmony with Gaia. After installing solar electric on my home in 1991, and watching the electric meter run backward as it fed sunlight into the grid, I felt the fundamental "rightness" of this vital technology that can turn sunlight into a stream of electrical energy.

Another area of opportunity for empathic design involves increased scaling down and localization of our food system.

While we have an active national movement supporting both locally grown foods sold through farmers markets and the humane treatment of animals raised for food, government-subsidized, corporate, industrial-scale agriculture remains firmly entrenched in much of the country producing the wheat, soybeans, and corn that are the basis for manufactured fast-food products. So many people seem to have lost contact with what real food is. Many Americans have no access to fresh fruits, vegetables, fish and meats. In poor urban districts, there are no stores within walking distance that carry fresh real foods. Such places are known as "food deserts." However, in cities such as Detroit, the loss of population and destruction of vacant homes are being replaced with food gardens and opportunities for encouraging people to grow some of their own food.

Over the years, I was engaged in developing and designing many food and garden projects, but I never seemed to have the time to grow my own. A few years ago, a friend in my community who had grown vegetables in her garden for thirty years offered a free series of Saturday classes called "Growing Gardeners" to anyone who wanted to learn. Her inspiring classes brought me to start my own backyard garden. It has been a deep learning experience leading me to a hands-on participation in the miracles of plant life cycles.

Many communities still have laws that prohibit growing anything other than grass on the front lawn. Historically, lawns were simply grassy fields not maintained by mowing machines but grazed by neighborhood sheep. The first "commons" were shared by the village neighborhood sheep. What an irony that the symbol of well-tended suburbia is a manicured green lawn. Homeowners need to come together to insist on more reasonable rules that would permit vegetable gardens on their property.

While the average age of farmers in the largely industrial farm belt is over sixty and their numbers keep diminishing, the number of young people interested in starting small organic vegetable farms is growing rapidly. The EcoFarm conference held every year at Asilomar in California attracted over thirteen hundred organic farmers in 2012, coinciding with a new US Department of Agriculture program providing loans to young beginning farmers. Another promising sign is the creation of Greenhorns, a fairly new national organization of young farmers that is active in providing information and assistance to this growing community.

Ocean Sunset—Japan

The number of farmers markets in the United States is growing exponentially, and leading restaurants and chefs are promoting local, organic, and seasonal foods. Another positive trend is that large wholesale food processors and distributors are being replaced by a new form: local food hubs where small farmers come together to aggregate, process, and market their own products directly to consumers. This complements Community Supported Agriculture (CSA), in which subscribing consumers receive a weekly box of freshly harvested produce.

New challenges to farming and all life systems are becoming more evident in our changing climate. Extreme droughts have plagued portions of the country and the world, and our economic system does not encourage water conservation. There are still many cities where water is essentially free and unmetered, as was the case in Sacramento for many years. The water supplied to California's agriculture flows through an elaborate, extensive, engineered system of dams and distribution systems, and is largely free to industrial agriculture, encouraging even greater waste. We must develop a relationship to water as a precious vital component of all life-forms. Society should reflect this in the design of its priority of uses, infrastructure, and pricing. We each have responsibility to value it and use it wisely.

The average American consumes 100 to 175 gallons of water per day. The average household use is 350 gallons per day or 130,000 gallons per year, and that number may not include outdoor sprinklers and automatic watering systems. As individuals, we Americans use far, far more water than do people in any other country, and the numbers don't include the much larger and even more wasteful use of water in large-scale mechanical agriculture, food processing, and raising animals for food.

Change in water use at the collective level is happening slowly. My own obsession, going back to the 1960s, was the flush toilet, the largest water user in homes. "Why?" I would ask myself, should we take one precious resource—water—and use it to flush away another precious resource—nutrient-rich human wastes—which after being dosed with chemicals in a sewage treatment plant, then foul another precious resource—our oceans, rivers, and lakes. Water-based sewage collection and treatment didn't begin until the early twentieth century. I advocated collecting and composting human wastes and then using them as a soil amendment. The first patented composting toilet was the Clivus Multrum in 1962, manufactured by a company owned by Abby Rockefeller, related to the first oil baron, John D. Rockefeller. We installed one in the Integral Urban House in Berkeley, and when the material processed itself naturally without water or chemicals, we used it in the garden. At the Farallones Rural Center in Occidental, California, I designed and built composting privies that are still in use forty years later. The decomposed material is composted with garden waste and used in the orchard.

When I was appointed California State Architect and director of the Governor's Office of Appropriate Technology in 1975, I continued to promote safe alternatives to "flush and forget." *The Toilet Papers: Recycling Waste and Conserving Water* was published in 1978 and became a favorite book of 1970s back-to-the-landers.[2] In 1976, a proposal to authorize a comprehensive study of alternative home sanitation systems was submitted to the Water Resources Control Board and signed by the directors of the State Health Department, the Department of Housing and Community Development, and the State Architect. I was able, during the three-year study period, to issue special permits allowing composting toilets and other ecologically innovative technologies such as greywater systems in our rural counties on an experimental basis.

At a larger scale, Humboldt County in Northern California wanted to spend fifty million dollars to build a new sewage system and treatment plant that would deposit its effluent into Humboldt Bay. They proposed to build the massive industrial facility on top of pristine wetlands. Wetlands are nature's biological filter to purify organic material. Working with biologists and ecologists at Humboldt State University, we proposed to build a constructed wetlands on the proposed site, which after primary treatment to settle out solids would use the wetlands to return biologically pure water to the bay and save the huge expense of the mechanical system first proposed.

Humboldt's Arcata Marsh, funded with state help, was an example that was copied in many other locations, reducing waste, pollution, and costs of sewage treatment in a sound ecological way. Waterless toilets are still exotic, although Seattle rewrote their codes to permit the six-story Bullitt Building to install composting toilets in its Living Building Challenge certified building.

Rainwater harvesting is another water-saving technology that is beginning to be taken seriously, particularly in regions stricken with drought. Australia has been a leader in the development of rainwater storage technologies using low, fireproof, steel-lined rather than plastic storage tanks. Consider the average 2,000-square-foot, one-story suburban house in a location where rainfall averages twelve inches per year. If all the water that fell on the roof from that one foot of rain were piped from gutters to a storage tank, that would be 150,000 gallons per year, more than the average household use. A circular storage tank four feet deep with a thirty-five-foot radius could store the year's water supply, and the need for stormwater systems would be eliminated.

Green roofs, first used in Germany on large flat-roofed buildings, are another way to eliminate the need for expensive stormwater systems as well as to reflect heat and absorb carbon. As climate chaos forces us to change the obsolete idea that clean water is endlessly available to waste, water-saving and ecologically sound solutions create the wave we need to save our future.

Having discussed opportunities for empathic realignment around how we relate to the basic elements of energy, food, and water, we turn to consider how our largely urban/suburban population can take the opportunity to begin, through empathy for self and others, to redesign shared and personal life systems.

The scientific and empirical consensus is that our entire planet is now living in and with global warming and climate chaos, which will continue to cause chaos for the eight billion people who live on Earth. Our life-supporting physical systems, which we have taken for granted—shelter, food, energy, water, waste, transportation—are not prepared for climate chaos. The probabilities of avoiding major breakdowns of the physical systems seem slim. The only thing that can replace our large rigid, unstable, and failing systems is human empathy, cooperation, and working together at every level, with the local community being the key. The 2012 Superstorm Sandy on the East Coast is an example of what we can expect. The local utility on Long Island, the Long Island Lighting Company (LILCO) took weeks to restore power because of poor management, lack of disaster readiness, and an aging, poorly maintained infrastructure. People helped each other, organizing neighborhood food and water distribution centers. People who had lost a lot helped neighbors who had lost everything.

As sociologist Eric Klinenberg writes in the *New Yorker* post-Sandy, social infrastructure is important to consider when deciding upon necessary infrastructure improvements for greater resilience in cities like New York.[3] In a letter to the editor in response to Klinenberg's article, Mark Hertsgaard, a longtime author on climate change issues, comments on the need for robust social infrastructure and tightly knit communities: "My interviews with scores of government officials, planners, scientists, and activists in various countries suggest that the most important elements of social infrastructure are the political, economic, and civil beliefs and practices that shape the way that societies address public issues. The Dutch lead the world in climate change adaptation largely because their history and geography move them to elevate the common good over individual interests."[4]

The extreme weather events of the recent years are a wake-up call. Rising sea levels and severe storms like Sandy will be more frequent and more severe. European countries like Holland have built extensive, sophisticated systems of levees to protect low-lying areas, but much of the US shoreline around dense cities such as Miami and New York remain unprotected. The Netherlands, where much of the country lies below sea level, is the international leader in hydraulic engineering. As a nation, we will have to make huge investments in holding back or diverting ocean waters. Much of our infrastructure—the electric energy grid, the highway and bridge systems, subways and trains, water and sewage systems—are obsolete and in need of upgrading or replacement.

Climate chaos, complex technologies, and overstretched supply and service lines create opportunities for people and communities to design working systems for themselves. Through cultivating community networks of resources and resourceful people, buying less, and doing more with local resources to maintain and conserve homes and communities, we become more self-reliant and our communities more resilient to the changes ahead.

Our building codes are largely written by corporations that benefit from new regulations. While codes are important to ensure human safety, they need to be written to respond to the new challenges and risks to our well-being raised by climate change. At the same time, much of our infrastructure—roads, bridges, transportation systems, underground utilities—are in need of repair and rebuilding, particularly in light of the increasing potential of flooding in many major urban areas. Our suburbs, our largest source of land and energy waste, need to be rebuilt to higher densities with more efficient systems, and also designed to create a greater sense of community.

Unfortunately, the dysfunction of nation-state governments in the United States and elsewhere, combined with irresponsible corporate greed and the disturbing ethic of people out for themselves, suggest that solutions toward more empathic environments will grow more from local efforts than from top-down centralized systems. Perhaps through necessity, adaptation and resiliency, combined with empathy and design, will merge to create a better future world. I will continue to grow my own food, share the surplus with neighbors, build micro solar energy grids in our community, and devote an hour each morning to join my neighbors in yoga practice with peace and gratitude.

Desertscape—New Mexico

6 | Journey to the Inner Self and Outer World

A human being is part of the whole called by us the universe, a part limited in time and space. We experience ourselves, our thoughts and feelings, as something separate from the rest, a kind of optical illusion of consciousness. . . . Our task must be to free ourselves from the prison by widening our circle of compassion to embrace all living creatures and the whole of nature in its beauty. . . . We shall require a substantially new manner of thinking if humanity is to survive.

—Albert Einstein

A QUALITY OF THE INNER SELF IS THAT IT PUTS US IN TOUCH WITH THE OUTER—experiencing the miracle of life itself in all its forms. The deeper you go into the true self, the closer you are to embodying a vision of the larger world that creates and maintains all life, a form of universal empathy. It is the bridge that recognizes our common humanity, and that we are all one. The great teachers who lived millennia ago offered something more radical than belief in a higher power. They offered a way of viewing reality that begins not with outside facts and a limited physical existence, but with inner wisdom and access to unbounded awareness. Carl Jung said, "Who looks outside, dreams, who looks within, awakens."

In *War of the Worldviews*, Deepak Chopra and Leonard Mlodinow debate over two seemingly opposing views of the world, science and spirituality. I believe these views can be complementary, as Einstein suggests. Chopra offers a passionate description of the issue, "In the spiritual worldview a hidden wholeness underlies all of creation, and ultimately it is this invisible wholeness that matters most. . . . Human consciousness created science, which ironically is now moving to exclude consciousness, its very creator. . . . To deny the worth of subjective experience is to dismiss most of what makes life worth living: love, trust, faith, beauty, awe, wonder, compassion, truth, the arts, morality, and the mind itself."[1]

How do we connect to our inner selves, the core of our being? How do we grow and feed it so that it nurtures us and allows us to nurture others and the natural world through design? Part of the problem may be that success in design tends to be measured by the celebrity status of well-known designers and the projection of their star qualities. They become role models for "good design," yet we really don't get to learn about what makes them tick or their inner nature. The brain does not control the inner spirit. You can't get a CAT scan of it, take a picture of it, or measure it with any technology, yet it is essential to our life and existence and to creating truly empathic design. It is our deepest connection to the magic, mystery, and wonder of being alive and connected to the endless and always changing stream of life within us and surrounding us. Without nurturing the inner self, people feel emptiness and a lack of meaning in their lives. Political journalist Norman Cousins, in the last days of his life, wrote with great poignancy, "Death is not the greatest loss in life. The greatest loss is what dies inside us while we live."[2]

Our scientific and technological world tends to dismiss phenomena that are beyond materiality. Earlier cultures, such as the Native Americans who inhabited North America for thousands of years before the arrival of white Europeans, understood themselves as part of the natural world in which they were embedded. They developed deep practices to honor the connection. For most of human history, cultures believed that humans and nature—trees, rocks, rivers—were all connected by a universally shared spirit and sense of the sacred.

Today we are not only living separate from a sense of unity with nature, but in a time of multiple interconnected crises—economic, political, and environmental. Our outer lives exist in a world that seems to be unraveling around us in all directions, leaving us tired, confused, and uncertain of our future. The only certainty today seems to be uncertainty about our collective future. That is why cultivating and nurturing an awareness of one's inner self is even more important now.

Discovering and nurturing the inner self is a different process for each individual. Everyone's journey toward an inner life will have its own path, and each person develops their own practices to cultivate their inner life. The essence is seeing life as a gift.

Cemetery—Oakland

The journey is important for anyone who believes that the meaning and purpose of their life extends beyond one's image, material success, and accomplishments, and it is essential for true empathic design. It is grounded in our connection to the timeless world of our soul and our spirit.

Let me briefly describe how experiences of my inner life have influenced my approach to design. Although I grew up in cities and suburbs, my first love was being outdoors in natural places. Most of my work is in places where nature is the foreground and not the background. I always try to integrate the basic natural elements of sun, earth, air, and water into the design so they tell the story of how they are related to the designed place and space. In our deepest being there is no separation between ourselves and everything else in the living world. Architecture by definition creates a separation, and our work must always be to find ways to let nature in. When I first visit the site of a new project, I sit and walk quietly for a day doing watercolor sketches of place. This I find is a way to literally embody the site and its spirit within me.

In recent years, I made the space and time to grow my own fruits and vegetables. Even though I had organized and designed many school and community garden projects, I had never felt I had time to participate in the experience I was helping to create for others.

Beginning thirty-five years ago, I started many food gardening projects in schools, communities, and learning centers because I believe food production is a key component of integrated design, which also includes water, waste management and recycling, renewable energy, community building, and education. The gardener/educators managing these gardens often suggested that I spend some time learning how to grow food. My usual reply was to smile, shrug my shoulders, and say, "That's a great idea except I don't have any time; I've got to raise money for these projects, make phone calls, manage the office. . . ." When I moved back up to the country seven years ago (after living on a houseboat in Sausalito, across the Golden Gate Bridge from San Francisco, for twenty-two years), I took the "Growing Gardeners" class from an old friend in our community who organized a well-attended free Saturday morning class taught by herself and other seasoned food gardeners in our region.

I finally had time to plant and tend a food garden, but it took a long time to connect my intellectual understanding of gardening to actual experience. Years ago, I had installed automatic sprinklers and drip irrigation in the raised beds where I planned to grow vegetables. Taking a walk with me through my newly planted garden, my teacher (I call her my Garden Goddess) told me, "You need to walk in your garden every day to see how things are doing." I replied, "But I don't know what I'm looking at or what I should be seeing." She smiled, "That's why you need to do it every day and it might be a good idea to water by hand so you can see how the plants respond." As I learned to grow my garden, I learned to grow my understanding of my inner self. It has taken a few years. Now I walk in my good-sized garden every morning, watering, talking to the growing plants, and experiencing the whole cycle of growth from seed to harvest, through food preparation and eating what we've grown.

Experiencing the full cycle of plant life I have tended from seeding through eating has deeply nurtured my inner being. For people in suburbs, and even cities, growing and consuming what seed, soil, sun, water, and care produces, puts us back in touch with an elemental life experience. It is ironic that today in our rich material/technological culture, most people never experience this basic truth of life, and are much the poorer for it in health and happiness. As home food gardening grows in this country, people are brought back to themselves and their senses. Growing a garden literally grounds us to the most basic truths of Mother Earth and ourselves. The whole cycle of planting, tending, and harvesting a garden, preparing food from what I have grown, and the pleasure of eating what I have nurtured, harvested, prepared, and consumed, brings me back to myself. Now, whenever possible, I suggest that edible and ornamental plants be integrated into the design.

My partner in gardening, yoga, and life says, "Yoga is like gardening. It nurtures body, mind, and soul." My most powerful experience toward nurturing the inner self has been in developing a regular practice of yoga. I did yoga forty years ago when the teachers focused only on getting the poses right. Today's teachers often incorporate the ancient wisdom from both the Hindu and the Buddhist philosophies into their teaching. My teachers stress the inner and outer benefits of yoga practice, especially coordinating *prana*, or breath, with the movement into a particular pose. I focus on each inhalation and exhalation as they move up and down the spine. My busy brain slows down and soon all I am aware of is the flow of breath and body movement. As our breath takes us into our inner being, our teacher relates stories from Hindu mythology, some of which focus on battles between the

Bristlecone Pine—Emigrant Basin, California

brain/mind and the heart. I have learned not only yoga positions but how breathing takes the focus away from the mind, bringing me back to my inner self.

The word *yoga* means "union"—a union with the higher self. In our culture today, the disconnect from others, from our deepest selves, and from nature is the root cause of the many problems our society and our country are experiencing. It has been a true blessing to discover yoga through my wonderful teachers and the community of people who share the practice every morning.

When I did a lot of deep body work (largely connected to my design work at Esalen Institute and the San Francisco Zen Center), I would develop very literal images of the body structure such as the rib cage, which did find their way into my design work. Gratitude and solitude are keystones to developing empathy and close relationships with clients, coworkers, and everyone involved in the design process. The overarching effect of developing an inner life is finding your own inner truth, and living by that. When people know and follow their inner truth in everything they do, the difficulties in life all become simply events in the stream of life. What research now shows is that expressing gratitude creates happiness both for you and for others.

All the data shows that the 1 percent of Americans who hold 90 percent of the country's wealth are no happier than the rest of us, except those that share some of their wealth for the common good. As Brother David Steindl-Rast, a Benedictine monk who has written extensively on gratefulness, says, "You can't be happy unless you are grateful. . . . Gratefulness is the shortest, simplest route to spirituality . . . knowing your own inner world is the primary valid view that needs no outside reflection."[3]

As a designer, I have always been driven to find solutions. Design solutions are far easier to find than solutions to the problems we face in our lives. I was often in two places: wherever I was in space and time, and wherever I was in my head. While I had a successful and gratifying life as a teacher and designer, I was often clueless to people's suffering and emotional states, including my family, colleagues, employees, and friends.

Our lives today remind me of fast-forwarding a movie download to four, eight, or sixteen times its normal speed. We race around, drowning in information and imagery. Next, next, next. Our eyes dart around, but are we truly seeing? With all our speedy need to get on with the next thing, we never catch up. Are we ever truly present? We're connected but how, to whom, what, why? To be present is to be gifted with the simple pleasures of peace and quiet, which seem the rarest of commodities in our present environment. A recent piece by Pico Iyer in the *New York Times* gives us a powerful picture of how our new information/communication technologies make finding that peace so much more difficult:

> *In barely one generation we've moved from exulting in the time-saving devices that have so expanded our lives to trying to get away from them—often in order to make more time. . . . A series of tests in recent years has shown, that after spending time in quiet rural settings, subjects exhibit greater attentiveness, stronger memory and generally improved cognition. Their brains become both calmer and sharper. . . . More than that, empathy, as well as deep thought, depends on neural processes that are 'inherently slow.' The very ones our high-speed lives have little time for.*[4]

What we're talking about is solitude, which except for my times alone painting or hiking, I had little of in my busy life. Reflecting on my life, it seems that I was not comfortable being alone for very long. These last few years are the first time in my life that I spend days in solitude. Yes, I read and answer e-mails, have friends over, stay in touch with family, and I'm active in our local community, but many days and nights I am alone, feeling comfortable and at peace without anxiety or worries. I am blessed with a wonderful partner and companion who is always in my heart, reminding me that while I am alone I am not lonely. We each enjoy our lives alone and also treasure our time together.

The deepest, most powerful form of empathy is intimacy with another human, a connection without boundaries set by the ego or the mind. An intimacy between two beings suggests that although each is a separate and unique individual, when they come together, their lives flow harmoniously in each present moment toward a larger whole.

I did not discover intimacy until late in life. My sense of empathy was directed toward large abstract human issues rather than specific individuals and situations. I now understand that my inability to be truly intimate was tied to a fear of abandonment and loss that I experienced in the early trauma of fleeing our homeland, which I discuss in my autobiography as well as in the preface to this book. As a child in a refugee family, we all suffered in silence. My parents did not share their pain. I now understand that the true test of intimacy and empathy is the ability for people to share their pain and suffering without fear of judgment. Fear—the opposite of compassion or empathy—drives our wants and addictions whether they be lusting for power, money, or fame, or fearing the inevitability of death.

You cannot find intimacy with another unless you can be truly intimate with yourself. In this book, I have tried to reconstruct my own journey of nurturing my inner self. Anything you do that truly nurtures the inner self is an exercise in developing intimacy with both yourself and others.

In my life, I have identified eight bridges into recurring points of connection to my inner self that live outside of linear time, flickering through my being without labels and shaping my inner

Boatyard—Sausalito

life. I urge you to search your inner being and discover your own list. Here is my lifetime list:

- an early love and feeling of connection to the natural world
- psychedelic experiences in nature
- watercolor painting in nature as a form of meditation
- growing a vegetable garden and communicating with the plants
- developing awareness of the inner self and outer body
- finding peace in solitude
- connection with others
- gratitude for the gift of life itself

Given the long period over which I absorbed and integrated these experiences into my inner being, there isn't a simple linear correlation to how they influenced my approach to design over these many years. Feeling a deep connection to nature developed through the first four experiences. Finding a deeper connection to my true self has been a process that coincided with major changes in my life over the past five years for which I am deeply grateful.

Notes

Preface

1. Gregory Bateson, *Mind and Nature: A Necessary Unity* (New York: Hampton Press, 2002), and *Steps to an Ecology of Mind: Collected Essays in Anthropology, Psychiatry, Evolution, and Epistemology* (Chicago: University of Chicago Press, 2000).

Chapter 1

1. Steve Jobs, Commencement speech at Stanford University, Palo Alto, CA, 2005.

2. Carlos Castenada, interview in *Intellectual Digest*, May 1972.

3. Sim Van der Ryn and Stuart Cowan, *Ecological Design* (Washington, DC: Island Press, 1996).

4. Sherry Turkle, *Alone Together: Why We Expect More from Technology and Less from Each Other* (New York: Basic Books, 2012).

5. Sigfried Giedion, *Mechanization Takes Command: A Contribution to Anonymous History* (New York: W.W. Norton, 1969).

6. Ernest Callenbach, "Ernest Callenbach, Last Words to an America in Decline," TomDispatch.com (posted May 6, 2012).

Chapter 2

1. Richard Farson, *The Power of Design: A Force for Transforming Everything* (Atlanta: Greenway Communications, 2008), 21.

2. Sim Van der Ryn and Murray Silverstein, "How Do Students Really Live?" *Architectural Forum* (July-August 1967): 91.

3. Sim Van der Ryn and Murray Silverstein, "Dorms at Berkeley: An Environmental Analysis," UC Center for Planning and Development Research, 1967.

4. Martin Trow and Michael Burrage, eds., *Twentieth Century Higher Education: Elite to Mass to Universal* (Baltimore: Johns Hopkins University Press, 2010), 305.

5. Ibid, 305.

6. Clare Cooper Marcus, *Easter Hill Village: Some Social Implications of Design* (New York: Free Press, 1975).

7. Oscar Newman, *Defensible Space: Crime Prevention Through Urban Design* (New York: Macmillian Publishing, 1973).

8. Jane Jacobs, *The Death and Life of Great American Cities* (New York: Random House, 1961).

9. Cathy Turner, *LEED Building Performance in the Cascadia Region: A Post Occupancy Evaluation Report* (Cascadia Region Green Building Council, January 30, 2006).

10. http://www.cbf.org/about-cbf.

11. Judith Heerwagen and Leah Zagreus, "The human factors of sustainable building design: post occupancy evaluation of the Philip Merrill Environmental Center," Indoor Environmental Quality (IEQ) Center for the Built Environment, Center for Design Research, UC Berkeley, April 1, 2005.

12. Ibid.

13. Farson, *The Power of Design*, 33.

14. Clare Cooper Marcus, "Social Factors in Architecture, 1960–2004," in Waverly Lowell, Elizabeth Byrne, and Betsy Frederick-Rothwell, eds., *Design on the Edge: A Century of Teaching Architecture at the University of California, Berkeley, 1903–2003* (University of California at Berkeley College of Environmental Design, 2009), 141.

15. Author phone interview with Aran Baker, January 2013.

16. Paula Baker-Laporte, Erica Elliott, and John Banta, *Prescriptions for a Healthy House: A Practical Guide for Architects, Builders & Homeowners*, 3rd edition (Gabriola Island, BC: New Society Publishers, 2008).

17. Environment and Human Health, Inc, "LEED Certification Where Energy Efficiency Collides with Human Health, An EHHI Report," http://www.ehhi.org/reports/leed/.

18. Baker-Laporte et al., *Prescriptions for a Healthy House.*

19. Ibid., page 25.

20. Ibid., page xxii.

21. http://www.paulabakerlaporte.com/articles/healthy-building/.

22. David E. Jacobs, Tom Kelly, and John Sobolewski, "Linking Public Health, Housing, and Indoor Environmental Policy: Successes and Challenges at Local and Federal Agencies in the United States," *Environmental Health Perspectives*, June 2007; 115(6): 976–82. Published online January 25, 2007, http://www.ncbi.nlm.nih.gov/pmc/articles/PMC1892139/.

23. Roger Barker, *Ecological Psychology: Concepts and Methods for Studying the Environment* (Stanford, CA: Stanford University Press, 1968).

24. Paul Goldberger, "Exclusive Preview: Google's New Built-from-Scratch Googleplex," *Vanity Fair*, February 22, 2013.

25. Ibid.

26. Ibid.

Chapter 3

1. See Edward O. Wilson, *Biophilia* (Cambridge, MA: Harvard University Press, 1984), and Stephen Kellert et al., eds., *The Biophilia Hypothesis* (Washington, DC: Island Press, 1995).

2. Sim Van der Ryn and Stuart Cowan, *Ecological Design* (Washington, DC: Island Press, 1996, pages 54–56).

3. James Howard Kunstler, *The Geography of Nowhere: The Rise and Decline of America's Man-Made Landscape* (New York: Simon and Schuster, 1993), 163.

4. Correspondence between Josiah Cain and Sim Van der Ryn, January 2013.

Chapter 4

1. Rob Fleming, *Design Education for a Sustainable Future* (London: Routledge, 2013).

2. Patrik Schumacher, "Schumacher Slams British Architectural Education," *Architectural Review*, 231 (February 2012): 92.

3. Sim Van der Ryn and the Farallones Institute, *Farallones Scrapbook: Making Places, Changing Spaces in Schools, at Home and within Ourselves* (Austin, TX: Book People, 1971).

4. Sim Van der Ryn, *Natural Energy Designer's Handbook* (New York: Random House, 1975).

5. Farallones Institute, Helga Olkowski, et al., *The Integral Urban House: Self-Reliant Living in the City* (San Francisco: Sierra Club Books, 1979).

6. http://samuelmockbee.net/rural-studio/about-the-rural-studio/.

7. http://www.yestermorrow.org/about-us/our-philosophy/.

8. http://www.solardecathlon.gov/index.html.

9. Correspondence between Island Press and Jason McLennan, February 19, 2013.

10. Jeremy Rifkin, *Empathic Civilization: The Race to Global Consciousness in a World in Crisis* (New York: Tarcher, 2009), 110.

11. Ernest L. Boyer and Lee D. Mitang, *Building Community: A New Future for Architecture Education and Practice*, (Princeton, NJ: The Carnegie Foundation for the Advancement of Teaching, 1996), 34.

12. Correspondence between Island Press and Tom Fisher, March 7, 2013.

Chapter 5

1. Sim Van der Ryn and California Governor Jerry Brown, speech at dedication of the Bateson Building, Sacramento, CA, September 1979.

2. Sim Van der Ryn, *The Toilet Papers: Recycling Waste and Conserving Water* (White River Junction, VT: Chelsea Green, 2008).

3. Eric Klinenberg, "Adaptation: How Can Cities Be 'Climate-Proofed'?," *The New Yorker*, January 7, 2013.

4. Mark Hertsgaard, "A letter in response to Eric Klinenberg's article," *The New Yorker*, February 4, 2013.

Chapter 6

1. Deepak Chopra and Leonard Mlodinow, *War of the Worldviews: Where Science and Spirituality Meet--and Do Not* (New York: Three Rivers Press, 2012).

2. Norman Cousins, http://www. thinkexist.com/quotes/norman_cousins/.

3. David Steindl-Rast, Gratefulness, *The Heart of Prayer* (Mahwah, NJ: Paulist Press, 1984).

4. Pico Iyer, "The Joy of Quiet," *New York Times*, Opinion, December 29, 2011.

About the Author

Sim Van der Ryn is president of the Ecological Design Collaborative, a design and consulting practice providing comprehensive design services. He has been at the forefront of integrating ecological principles into the built environment, creating multiscale solutions driven by nature's intelligence for over forty years. A professor of architecture at the University of California, Berkeley for thirty-five years, he served as California's first energy-conscious State Architect, authored seven influential books, including *Ecological Design* (Island Press 1995), and won numerous honors and awards for his leadership and innovation in architecture and planning, including the 2008 Athena Award for Lifetime Achievement, Congress for New Urbanism; Rockefeller Scholar in Residence, Bellagio, Italy (1997 and 2013); a Commendation for Excellence in Technology, California Council American Institute of Architects (1981); and a Guggenheim Fellowship (1971). He is Emeritus Professor of Architecture and Environmental Design at the University of California, Berkeley.

Index

Illustrations are indicated by an "f".

About Island Press

Since 1984, the nonprofit Island Press has been stimulating, shaping, and communicating the ideas that are essential for solving environmental problems worldwide. With more than 800 titles in print and some 40 new releases each year, we are the nation's leading publisher on environmental issues. We identify innovative thinkers and emerging trends in the environmental field. We work with world-renowned experts and authors to develop cross-disciplinary solutions to environmental challenges.

Island Press designs and implements coordinated book publication campaigns in order to communicate our critical messages in print, in person, and online using the latest technologies, programs, and the media. Our goal: to reach targeted audiences—scientists, policymakers, environmental advocates, the media, and concerned citizens—who can and will take action to protect the plants and animals that enrich our world, the ecosystems we need to survive, the water we drink, and the air we breathe.

Island Press gratefully acknowledges the support of its work by the Agua Fund, Inc., The Margaret A. Cargill Foundation, Betsy and Jesse Fink Foundation, The William and Flora Hewlett Foundation, The Kresge Foundation, The Forrest and Frances Lattner Foundation, The Andrew W. Mellon Foundation, The Curtis and Edith Munson Foundation, The Overbrook Foundation, The David and Lucile Packard Foundation, The Summit Foundation, Trust for Architectural Easements, The Winslow Foundation, and other generous donors.

The opinions expressed in this book are those of the author(s) and do not necessarily reflect the views of our donors.